PRESENTED TO

_____

ON THE OCCASION OF

_____

Hayley, nothing has challenged me more to think deeply about you,

your character, and our marriage than co-writing this book.

I am broken that the Lord would bless a man

as unworthy as me with a wife as excellent as you.

I am beyond thankful to Him that

"I found the one I love" (Song of Solomon 3:4). ILYF.

BRAD

*Carina, it is hard to put in a few words what you have meant
to me over these years. You have been Christlike in your faithfulness
and forgiveness to me. God has used you to spur me on to greater holiness
as I have witnessed a consistent Proverbs 31 life in you.
You are the perfect helpmate for me. To God be the glory for His providence.*

RUSS

GREAT IS GOD'S FAITHFULNESS . . .

AND YOURS AS WELL. THANK YOU, MIKE.

I LOVE YOU.

LISA

No Greater **Love**
© 2010 by Coram Deo Studios Inc.

Published in Nashville, Tennessee, by Thomas Nelson. Thomas Nelson is a trademark of Thomas Nelson, Inc.

Designed by Koechel Peterson Design, Minneapolis, MN

Managing Editor: Lisa Stilwell

Thomas Nelson, Inc., titles may be purchased in bulk for educational, business, fund-raising, or sales promotional use. For information, please e-mail SpecialMarkets@ThomasNelson.com.

Unless otherwise noted, all Scripture references are from the NEW KING JAMES VERSION. © 1982, 1992, by Thomas Nelson, Inc. All rights reserved.

Other Scripture references are taken from the NEW AMERICAN STANDARD BIBLE® (NASB), © the Lockman Foundation 1960, 1962, 1963, 1968, 1971, 1972, 1973, 1975, 1977, 1995. Used by permission. HOLY BIBLE: NEW INTERNATIONAL VERSION® (NIV). © 1973, 1978, 1984 International Bible Society. Used by permission of Zondervan Publishing House. All rights reserved. THE ENGLISH STANDARD VERSION (ESV). © 2001 by Crossway Bibles, a division of Good News Publishers. Used by Permission.

ISBN-13: 978-1-4041-8778-8 (hardcover)
ISBN-13: 978-1-4003-2316-6 (paperback)

Printed in the United States of America

NO
GREATER
LOVE

a 90-day
devotional
for couples

RUSS W. RICE | BRAD J. SILVERMAN | LISA GUEST

THOMAS NELSON
Since 1798

NASHVILLE DALLAS MEXICO CITY RIO DE JANEIRO

CONTENTS

FOREWORD

IN THE EARLY 1970S, I learned a lesson that has shaped my life and ministry in a profound way.

When I graduated from college in 1970, I joined the staff of Campus Crusade for Christ. My own life had been marked by Campus Crusade during my years in college, and I wanted to be part of helping to fulfill the Great Commission (Matthew 28:19–20).

My first ministry assignment was in Dallas, Texas, where I shared Christ with high school students and discipled those who came to faith. What I had not anticipated was that one of the biggest obstacles I would face in trying to help students grow in Christ was their home environment.

I grew up in a small town in southern Missouri. My dad ran the local gas company. My mom took care of my brother and me. Our family wasn't perfect, by any stretch of the imagination. But I never doubted that my parents loved me. And I never doubted their love for each other.

And I thought everybody's family was just like mine.

When I started working with high school students, I quickly learned that behind the four walls of the homes in affluent neighborhoods in North Dallas, families were in trouble. And most often, the families were in trouble because marriages were in trouble.

I realized before long that if I really wanted to help high school students, the best thing I could do for them was to help their moms and dads.

Strong, healthy families are the foundation of every stable society. And strong marriages are the headwaters of every strong family.

I have invested more than three decades of my life now in helping couples build stronger marriages and families. What has always been obvious to me is that strong families and strong marriages find their ultimate strength in the spiritual foundation upon which they are built.

That's what Jesus said in Matthew 7:24–27. "Everyone then who hears these words of mine and does them will be like a wise man who built his house on the rock. And the rain fell, and the floods came, and the winds blew and beat on that house, but it did not fall, because it had been founded on the rock. And everyone who hears these words of mine and does not do them will be like a foolish man who built his house on the sand. And the rain fell, and the floods came, and the winds blew and beat against that house, and it fell, and great was the fall of it" (ESV).

This book will help you fortify the foundation of your home. It is more than a book to read. It's an action plan for having the kind of marriage that stands strong when the storms of life come. A marriage that provides your family with a stable, healthy home. A marriage that provides the foundation for a stable society.

And above all else, a marriage that honors and glorifies God.

When Barbara and I were first married, the best advice we received came from a couple who were a few laps ahead of us on the marriage track. They challenged us to pray together every day as a couple. That's a discipline we have worked to preserve in our relationship.

I want to pass that challenge on to you. Use this book as a catalyst in your marriage to cultivate the habit of daily prayer together as a couple.

Our love for one another in marriage will run dry unless we are connected to a source of love that is greater than ourselves. God's love for us, seen clearly in the sacrifice of Jesus to liberate us from our slavery to sin, is the only source of love that never fails. 1 John 4:19 says, "We love because He first loved us" (ESV).

And truly there is "no greater love."

Dennis Rainey | President, *FamilyLife*

INTRODUCTION

"I DO."

Small words. Big beyond-imagining joys—and challenges.

"In sickness, and in health . . . in plenty, and in want . . . for better, for worse . . ."

Few, if any, brides or grooms have any idea what they're really getting into.

And in the same vein, we simply had no idea how the Lord would challenge each of us as we embarked on writing this book.

As the three of us prayerfully labored to accurately understand, concisely explain, and wisely apply the life-changing truths dealt with in this devotional, God has used His Word to renew our minds and positively transform our marriages.

With the writer of Hebrews, we believe the Bible is "living and active. Sharper than any double-edged sword, it penetrates even to dividing soul and spirit, joints and marrow; it judges the thoughts and attitudes of the heart" (Hebrews 4:12 NIV). We also believe the Word of God is without error (Psalm 19:7) and is our final authority in all matters of life (Psalm 119:89).

So it should go without saying that we believe the keys to a successful and fulfilling marriage are found in none other than the Holy Scriptures.

Just as the Lord has touched our lives as we've written this book, it is our prayer that, as you and your spouse dedicate a few minutes each day to reading a devotional together, God's Word will shine through and the Holy Spirit will work in your hearts to make you more like Him and more the husband and wife He has called you to be.

At the conclusion of each devotional, you will find a special section we've titled "Love in Action." These real-life, practical points of discussion and application are designed to encourage and solidify both your marriage and your personal walks with God. If you don't get to every Love in Action activity, please don't feel defeated. In fact, we pray that every aspect of this book will draw you to a deeper intimacy with our loving Father, as well as encourage you to a greater love and commitment to the life-mate the Lord has graciously given you—your spouse.

May the Lord use this book to richly bless your marriage.

All our love in Christ,

Russ Rice | Brad Silverman | Lisa Guest

NOW THAT IS GOOD!

Then God saw everything that He had made,
and indeed it was very good.

GENESIS 1:31

PULLING THE PAPER THIS way, folding it that way, Susie was hard at work. Her little hands didn't find the task easy, and she was concentrating as hard as a six-year-old can. Finally, with a little smile, she lifted her special creation and said, "Look! Isn't it good?"

God gave us the ability to be creative, but He is the Creator of all things. In six literal days He created all things, including man.

* He created light and darkness on the first day (Genesis 1:3–4).
* Next, He created the heavens (vv 6–8).
* On day three, God created the sea and the earth, the plants and the trees (vv 9–13).
* He created the sun, moon, and stars on the fourth day (vv 14–19).
* On the fifth day He created the fish and the birds (vv 20–23).
* And on the sixth day, He created the animals and man (vv 24–27).

And God saw everything He had made, and indeed it was very good (v 1:31).

Look out your window at the sky, the trees, the people—He created it all from nothing.

But, you're wondering, *what does this have to do with marriage?* Good question.

Notice that the list above is hardly comprehensive; an important thing is missing. As Genesis 2:20 says, "But for Adam there was not found a helper suitable for him" (NASB). God created man, but He wanted something better than a bunch of monkeys for man to hang around with. So God created woman out of Adam's rib, and Adam was breath-taken-away excited about her.

God, in His goodness, gave Adam the most suitable mate possible: she was bone of his bone and flesh of his flesh. And God, in His goodness, has done the same for you.

> THANK YOU, CREATOR GOD, FOR KNOWING WHAT WE HUMAN BEINGS NEED IN A COMPANION. THE HEAVENS YOU CREATED DECLARE YOUR GLORY! THE SPOUSE YOU CREATED AND GAVE TO ME DECLARES YOUR LOVE! I'M HUMBLED BY AND GRATEFUL FOR THE GIFT OF MY SPOUSE. THANK YOU, FATHER.

People travel to wonder at the height of the mountains, at the huge waves of the seas, and yet they pass by themselves without wondering.

ST. AUGUSTINE

LOVE IN ACTION

1. Head to the nearby zoo or aquarium and marvel at God's creation. During your day of fun, don't forget to marvel at the amazing creation you have personally received from God—your spouse!

2. Write a love note to your spouse. It doesn't need to be long, but take this opportunity to think about the blessing that your mate is.

GOD GAVE ME YOU

*Then Isaac brought her into his mother Sarah's tent; and he took
Rebekah and she became his wife, and he loved her.*

GENESIS 24:67

* Mark and Ann met on a blind date.
* Scott and Jennifer met in high school.
* Mike and Lisa met in college—and then again eight years later.

THE LORD WORKS IN mysterious ways, and the story of how you met
may reflect the mystery of His working in your lives.

As you think back on your story, you can probably point to
those moments that cemented your conviction that God had brought you
together. The songwriters would play up the romance, and the cynics would
credit fate. But the psalmist has it right when he marvels, "Your eyes saw
my unformed body. All the days ordained for me were written in your book
before one of them came to be" (Psalm 139:16 NIV).

God brought the two of you together, and you have vowed—before
Him and before many faithful witnesses—to stay together. And you've
weathered the family camping trip when the kids threw up on all the sleeping
bags. You've weathered the job layoff and the skin cancer scare. And
you've weathered how many family gatherings?

Now, to celebrate the storms you've survived, how 'bout going to one of
your favorite dating destinations? Revisiting that significant spot might be
a fun reminder to you both that "God gave me you!"

> THANK YOU, LORD GOD, THAT EVEN AS YOU KEEP
> THE PLANETS IN THEIR ORBITS, YOU CARE ENOUGH
> ABOUT OUR HEARTS, OUR LIVES, OUR GROWTH INTO
> CHRISTLIKENESS THAT YOU GIVE US EACH OTHER FOR
> THE JOURNEY. JUST AS YOU GAVE REBEKAH TO ISAAC,
> LET US CHERISH EACH OTHER. HELP US BE MORE
> THANKFUL AND APPRECIATIVE AS WE REMEMBER THAT
> OUR SPOUSE IS A GIFT FROM YOU.

When we receive any good to our souls or to our bodies, whoever is the instrument, let us look to the Principal; as in the gifts we receive, we look not to him that brings but to him who sent them.

RICHARD
SIBBES

LOVE IN ACTION

1. Think back to your dating days and the reasons you knew that your spouse was *The One*. On a date, talk about some of those words or actions that helped you know that God's plan was for you two to be together.

2. What are some of the storms you've already weathered? What enabled you to do so? What are you doing to be sure those factors are in place for the next storm?

OMNISCIENT, ETERNAL, AND OMNIPOTENT

"I am the Alpha and the Omega,
the Beginning and the End," says the Lord, "who is
and who was and who is to come, the Almighty."

REVELATION 1:8

L IFE IS DIFFICULT, AND marriage may be the greatest challenge you have ever faced. But before you're tempted to think you're in it alone, let's remember three awesome attributes about the incredibly intimate God who brought you two together.

God is *Omniscient.* The expression "the Alpha and the Omega," referring to the first and last letters of the Greek alphabet, tells us that God knows all things; not one iota of knowledge is beyond Him.

Right now, stare at your spouse right in the eyes for ten seconds, but don't say a word. Do you know *exactly* what your spouse is thinking? God does.

God is *Eternal.* The God we can turn to when we are painfully aware of our human limitations has no beginning, and He has no end.

He not only existed from the beginning of time—He existed before there *was* time—He created time. Chew on that one for a minute!

God is *Omnipotent.* He controls all things and upholds all things by His power. No thing or person or situation, not Satan or death, can overtake Him or hold Him. God is almighty, all powerful.

For I am persuaded that neither death nor life, nor angels nor principalities nor powers, nor things present nor things to come, nor height nor depth, nor any other created thing, shall be able to separate us from the love of God which is in Christ Jesus our Lord (Romans 8:38–39).

> LORD GOD, YOU ARE OMNISCIENT, ETERNAL, AND OMNIPOTENT—AND YOU CARE ABOUT OUR MARRIAGE. THANK YOU FOR NOT CARING FROM AFAR, BUT FOR COMING NEAR TO HELP US WHEREVER WE NEED YOUR WISDOM AND STRENGTH.

How should finite comprehend infinite? We shall apprehend Him, but not comprehend Him.
RICHARD SIBBES

LOVE IN ACTION

1. What situation in your life or, more specifically, in your marriage relationship does this discussion of God's omniscience, eternal nature, and omnipotence speak to?

2. Go through the alphabet, A to Z, and take turns saying a word starting with that letter that describes the Lord. **A**lmighty, **B**oundless, **C**aring . . . You'll probably laugh when you try to think of a Q and an X . . . Praise Him anyway!

YOUR INSTRUCTION MANUAL . . . FOR LIFE

*His divine power has given to us all things
that pertain to life and godliness, through the knowledge
of Him who called us by glory and virtue.*

2 PETER 1:3

INSTRUCTION MANUALS. SOME FOLKS wouldn't dream of plugging something in or beginning assembly work until reading that little book from cover to cover. Others think, "If I get stuck, I'll see what the manual has to say." And still others throw it away faster than they can open the box of the thing that the manual instructs them about.

Whatever your practice may be with manuals, one thing is certain: a clear, thorough, step-by-step instruction guide written by the very person who created that recent purchase would probably be helpful.

Well, our Creator God, the One who created you and your spouse, has given us such a manual—the Bible. But this instruction book is not only helpful, it is essential. In it is guidance for any and every situation we will encounter in life. In its pages is all the truth we need to receive the blessings of eternal salvation, on how to live a righteous life, and even how to love our spouse.

What a great encouragement to know that in His Word, the Lord has given us all things that pertain to life and godliness.

So don't throw out His instruction manual. Instead, read it, study it, meditate on it, and then do it—as a first resort, not the last!

> LORD, IT MAKES SENSE THAT YOUR WORD IS AN
> INSTRUCTION MANUAL FOR MY LIFE, FOR OUR
> MARRIAGE. PLEASE HELP ME, LORD, TO READ THAT
> MANUAL AND DO WHAT IT SAYS.

LOVE IN ACTION

1. This week find two or three opportunities to encourage your spouse with a Scripture verse. Does he need to be reminded of the Lord's strength? Does she need to hear about His love for her?

2. Each of you choose two or three verses from the Bible. Then memorize a verse a week. Hold each other accountable and plan a reward system like back rubs every day for a week for the first one who nails it. Hiding God's Word in our heart helps us draw on God's wisdom and not our own.

I have convenanted with my Lord that he should not send me visions or dreams or even angels. I am content with this gift of the Scriptures, which teaches and supplies all that is necessary, both for this life and that which is to come.
MARTIN LUTHER

ROAD MAP FOR MARRIAGE
| PART 1 |

A man will leave his father and mother and be united to his wife,
and they will become one flesh.

GENESIS 2:24 NIV

L ET'S PULL INTO THE gas station and get directions."

"No. I don't need directions. We can figure this out."

Yes, this brief exchange is stereotypical and—in this day of MapQuest and GPS—perhaps outdated. But that short discussion does reveal two distinctly different opinions about the value of directions. Do we need directions from someone who knows the area—or don't we?

God's design is for you to be united with your spouse, in a one-flesh union, for life. He has not only decreed this, but He has also given us the map we need to successfully travel this path together—the Bible! Consider these basic principles:

* "Submit to one another out of reverence for Christ."
   —Ephesians 5:21 NIV
* "Let each one of you [husbands] in particular so love his own wife as himself, and let the wife see that she respects her husband." —
   Ephesians 5:33
* "Love suffers long and is kind . . . does not behave rudely, does not seek its own [way], is not provoked, thinks no evil . . . bears all things, believes all things, hopes all things, endures all things."
   —1 Corinthians 13:4–7

Are you on God's road for your marriage?

> LORD, PLEASE HELP US KEEP OUR EYES ON YOU AS WE TRAVEL THIS MARRIAGE ROAD. HELP US TO STAY ON YOUR PATH AND TO REMEMBER, ESPECIALLY DURING THE TIMES WHEN WE WANT TO GO OUR OWN WAY, THAT YOU KNOW THE BEST ROUTE FOR A STRONG AND LASTING MARRIAGE THAT HONORS YOU.

As God by creation made two of one, so again by marriage He made one of two.
THOMAS ADAMS

LOVE IN ACTION

1. What couple do you know who serves as a good role model for a godly marriage? What do you appreciate about what you see? Get together with them and tell them what you admire and respect about their marriage. Then ask them to tell you where, if at all, they see you straying from God's road map.

2. What tips for a godly marriage do you wish you'd heard before you said, "I do"? God can help you incorporate those into your marriage even now. Ask Him to help you live out what you have learned about marriage from His road map and His people.

ROAD MAP FOR MARRIAGE
| PART 2 |

All Scripture is given by inspiration of God,
and is profitable for doctrine, for reproof, for correction,
for instruction in righteousness, that the man of God
may be complete, thoroughly equipped for every good work.

2 TIMOTHY 3:16–17

I'T'S DATE NIGHT. YOU'RE looking forward to a nice evening, but you need to bring up a difficult subject.

Now fast forward to the end of the day. How did it go? Was your prayer like this: "Lord, as good a day as it was, as nice a date night as we tried to have, everything would have been better if I'd spent time in Your Word and listened for You to guide my words and my tongue. Thank You for being faithful to me even though I'm less than faithful to You."

Or like this: "God, that was a tough conversation we had over dinner, but it was cool that what I read in my quiet time this morning helped so much! Thanks for going before us, so we could talk through the issue. I shudder to think how that conversation would have gone—and how our relationship would have been affected—if You hadn't guided me through Your Word."

How often do you consult the road map for marriage that God has provided? Do you ever open God's Word together and let it do its transforming work in stereo?

As Paul taught in the verse above, Scripture instructs us and corrects us so that we can be "thoroughly equipped for every good work." Marriage gives us opportunities to do good works 24/7, and God's Word prepares us to seize those opportunities. Scripture shows us where we fall short of God's standards and how to live a righteous life in our home. And Scripture reminds us that we can only live the way God wants us to live if we are living in His power.

> FATHER, IT WOULD BE CRAZY FOR US TO GO INTO UNEXPLORED TERRITORY WITHOUT A MAP, YET EVERY NEW SEASON, EVERY NEW DAY OF MARRIAGE IS UNEXPLORED TERRITORY. IN PREPARATION FOR THOSE SEASONS, AS WELL AS FOR EVERYDAY GUIDANCE IN OUR MARRIAGE, HELP US TO MAKE READING THE BIBLE A PRIORITY, INDIVIDUALLY AND AS A COUPLE.

LOVE IN ACTION

1. What are the biggest obstacles to the two of you doing a Bible study together? Lack of time? Not knowing what to study? Wanting to join a group but not being able to find one? Discuss what the obstacles are and decide together what you will do to overcome them.

2. Remember the couple you mentioned earlier, the couple that provides you with a good role model for a godly marriage? Ask them what role Bible study—either separately or together—plays in their marriage. Pray about following their example for your own.

The Christian is bred by the Word, and he must be fed by it.
WILLIAM GURNALL

DON'T GO IT ALONE!

*Let us consider one another
in order to stir up love and good works,
not forsaking the assembling of ourselves together.*

HEBREWS 10:24–25

* "It's the last game of the season. Of *course* I'm going."
* "It's my favorite show. I'll never miss it."
* "Work has been so stressful. I need my weekends to relax."

MOST OF US WOULD agree that life is pretty busy. Not only do we have our responsibilities at work and around the home, but we are bombarded with so many options as to how to spend what little "free" time we have. Should we go to the movies? Watch a game? Maybe do some shopping? And let's not get started with the kids' activities. There are so many choices, and so little time.

But what *should* be our priority? As long as we get our work done, does it really matter how we spend our time?

Our passage today gives us our priority: members of the body of Christ should be getting together on a regular basis. And not only for fun and games, though there's a time for that, but for the purpose of encouraging one another in our relationship and walk with the Lord.

The most obvious place to meet is the church. Regular attendance and participation is vital for the success and effectiveness of community outreach and for our overall worship. There are also small group settings in homes where couples can really connect with, minister to, pray for, and serve with other couples on a deeper level.

We may not always think so, but each of us has much to give the church, and God has designed all of us to be an integral part of the body (1 Corinthians 12:14–18).

So let's make being with other believers a priority. And if your neighbors see you and think, "They always go to church," take it as a compliment as to how much you love God's children!

LORD GOD, YOU ARE VERY MUCH A PART OF OUR RELATIONSHIP, AND WE KNOW THAT YOU DESIGNED US TO NEED THE BODY OF CHRIST. PLEASE GIVE US A GREAT DESIRE FOR THE TYPE OF FELLOWSHIP THAT WILL ENCOURAGE OUR LOVE FOR YOU AS WELL AS FOR EACH OTHER.

To gather with God's people in united adoration of the Father is as necessary to the Christian life as prayer.
MARTIN LUTHER

LOVE IN ACTION

1. What are you involved in at church that helps strengthen your marriage? In what ways has that involvement—whether you're serving together or attending a class together—helped you remember why you love your spouse?

2. In addition to church, what are some other ways you can spend time with fellow believers? Inviting a family for dinner? Planning an activity together? Pick one, make it happen, and enjoy the fellowship!

MARRIED—FOR LIFE

"Have you not read that... 'A man shall leave his father and mother and be joined to his wife, and the two shall become one flesh'? Consequently they are no longer two, but one flesh. What therefore God has joined together, let no man separate."

MATTHEW 19:4–6

DOES IT STRIKE YOU as odd that we human beings are arrogant enough to think that we can redefine marriage? that we can pass laws establishing marriage as other than a relationship between a man and a woman? or that we can define marriage between a man and a woman as nothing more than a temporary, as-long-as-you-meet-my-needs relationship?

No matter what legislative and judicial bodies do today, they can't alter the truth that marriage is a God-ordained institution dating back to Adam and Eve in the garden. It was there He established marriage as a relationship between one man and one woman . . . for life.

Sadly, the divorce rate in the church has slowly caught up to that of the general public. The rough seasons in a marriage—and those seasons can be very rough and can seem quite hopeless—are an opportunity for us to grow individually in our faith as we rely on God to help us be true to our covenant vows. If you are in such a spot right now, remember that nothing is impossible for Him (see Luke 1:37).

FATHER, THANK YOU FOR CREATING OUR MARRIAGE TO BE A LIFE LONG, "ONE FLESH" UNION. HELP US TO REMEMBER THAT NO ONE IS TO SEPARATE WHAT YOU HAVE JOINED TOGETHER— NOT EVEN US. MAY WE TRULY REJOICE IN KNOWING THAT EVEN WHEN SEASONS LOOK HOPELESS, WITH YOUR STRENGTH WE CAN NOT ONLY SURVIVE IN OUR MARRIAGE, BUT THRIVE.

Even a temporary separation should be the last resource, and every possible effort made to avoid such a tragedy.
A.W. PINK

LOVE IN ACTION

1. Talk about the factors that have kept you together through the years—and thank God for those.

2. Perhaps with a trusted third party present to mediate and pray with you, talk openly about the factors that are interfering with your relationship, that are robbing you of the oneness and joy that God intends marriage to bring to a husband and wife.

JUST SAY NO!

*"For the LORD God of Israel says that He hates divorce,
For it covers one's garment with violence," says the LORD of hosts.*

MALACHI 2:16

YES, GOD HATES DIVORCE. It goes completely against His divine design for the men and women He created. God knows what is best for us human beings, and His commands direct us to follow His path, a path He has outlined for our own good.

Yet even when we're exactly where God wants us to be—and once we say, "I do," we're where God wants us to be—the path isn't necessarily easy. Simply put, marriage is one of the greatest tools God uses to bring out our sin—our downfalls and shortcomings—and it exposes our self-centeredness like few other experiences can. And who of us wants to look at our negative traits when it's so much easier to go the opposite direction and run—from God and the relationship?

At the same time, Satan loves to dangle the idea of divorce in our minds as a foothold for his deceitful attacks. He knows that pondering the thought of divorce as an option can change (and weaken) our approach to problem solving. And his success in this approach is obvious given the divorce rate now.

The good news is, our God is a God of amazing power and grace, and by His strength and the support of the church and fellow believers, you and your spouse *can* work through the seemingly insurmountable marital challenges and the most painful of hurts. Lean on Him and His Word with all your hearts—and trust Him to be faithful to you in return.

> LORD, WE MADE A COVENANT PROMISE TO YOU TO STAY TOGETHER UNTIL DEATH DO US PART. WHEN KEEPING THAT PROMISE GETS TOUGH—AND IT WILL FROM TIME TO TIME—PLEASE SURROUND US AND PROTECT US FROM THE ENEMY'S ATTEMPTS TO PULL US APART. POUR YOUR GRACE AND SUPERNATURAL POWER INTO OUR HEARTS AND MINDS, THAT WE MIGHT WEATHER THE STORM FOR YOUR GLORY AND OUR GOOD.

LOVE IN ACTION

1. Take a walk together. Hold hands. Think out loud together about the cost of divorce—the cost for each of you, your children, the grandparents, your friends, the church. As you walk along, ask God to protect your marriage and to grow your love for Him and for each other.

2. Talk to God about how He has used your spouse to reveal your sin so you can confess it and He can make you more like Christ. Thank Him for that important aspect of marriage.

Marriage is not a mere civil thing, but is partly spiritual and Divine, and therefore God alone has the power to appoint the beginning, the continuance, and the end thereof.
A.W. PINK

Reality Check

THE BRIDE WAS RADIANT . . .
Her bridesmaids fought back tears of joy . . .
The groom was tall and confident . . .
His attendants smiled their support . . .
The music was joyous and bright . . .
The flowers were fresh and fragrant . . .

The stage was set for a glorious wedding, and the expectations for the couple's future together were high. Who would get married if that weren't the case?

But expectations—fueled by dreams and movies, by ignorance and youth—can go unfulfilled. If we expect our marriage to always feel happily ever after, we are in for a rude awakening—like Mary Poppins meets Terminator.

So what do we do? Where do we turn when there's no hope for the perpetual fairy tale?

King David was a man who knew where to place his hope. He knew the only true hope he had was found in the Lord, and Him alone. The only expectation David had in his life and for his future was that God would be faithful and He would always keep His promises.

In marriage, we need to be careful where we place our hope. Like David, we need to fix our expectations only on the promises of our never-changing, all-loving God. And as we do this, we will grow to love and praise Him more and more as we see His faithfulness continually shine through.

Say goodbye to the fairy tale. Put all your hope in the Lord, who is worthy of our trust and who never disappoints!

> GOD OF WONDER, PLEASE HELP ME TO NOT PUT UNFAIR
> EXPECTATIONS ON MY SPOUSE. I PRAY THAT YOU WOULD
> HELP ME BETTER UNDERSTAND THAT ALL MY HOPE SHOULD
> BE PLACED IN YOU AND YOUR WORD, AND PLEASE GIVE ME
> THE KIND OF HOPE THAT KINDLES EXCITEMENT FOR WHAT
> YOU WILL DO IN MY HEART AND IN MY MARRIAGE.

LOVE IN ACTION

1. Think about your wedding day. Talk together about what was going through your mind about the future. Remember together the dreams you shared. Then list at least three areas that God has blessed you in ways far greater than you could have asked or imagined.

2. Think about those expectations you had, if any, that resulted in disappointment or despair and re-evaluate them. Were they realistic? Ask forgiveness for the stress or distress any unfair expectations may have brought to the marriage.

Do not look to your hope, but to Christ, the source of your hope.
CHARLES SPURGEON

IT'S NOT ALL ABOUT YOU

For to me, to live is Christ, and to die is gain.

PHILIPPIANS 1:21

S O HOW LONG DID the honeymoon last for you? Years, months—or minutes?

Sometimes what cuts short the honeymoon period of a marriage is when one or both of the newlyweds come to the startling realization that marriage is not all about him or her.

The truth is, life in general is not all about any one of us. The apostle Paul knew life wasn't all about him. According to Philippians 1:21, Paul knew that life was all about Jesus Christ—to Paul, "to *live* [was] Christ." Nothing has changed in the past two thousand years. Today, like in Paul's day, a life lived to the fullest is one that is lived fully for Christ. In order to do this, however, we must die to ourselves.

Think about it. If both husband and wife die to self, fully die to selfishness and pride, and live wholeheartedly for Jesus, just imagine what an awesome, blessing-filled marriage it would be!

Paul followed "to live is Christ" with "to die is gain." In other words, in addition to the loving, joyful, peaceful marriage you will experience in this life, you can know that you and your spouse will experience God's immeasurable blessings for all eternity, and this is surely *gain!*

> LORD GOD, YOU KNOW EVEN BETTER THAN I DO THOSE
> STRONGHOLDS IN MY LIFE WHERE I STILL LIVE AS IF LIFE
> WERE ALL ABOUT ME. PLEASE REVEAL THEM TO ME AND
> HELP ME TO DIE TO MY SELFISH WAYS SO THAT I MAY FULLY
> LIVE FOR YOU IN ALL AREAS OF MY LIFE.

They lose nothing who gain Christ.

SAMUEL RUTHERFORD

LOVE IN ACTION

1. Talk (and laugh?) together about the first reminder you received as a married person that this marriage is not all about you. (Are you smiling?)

2. "A life lived to the fullest is one that is lived fully for Christ." Reflect and pray through this concept together. Ask God to show you if there are areas in your marriage that can be lived even more fully for Him. Then give each other a big kiss!

THE PETER PAN PRINCIPLE

A foolish son is a grief to his father,
and bitterness to her who bore him.

PROVERBS 17:25

"DID NOT!"

"He started it!"

"I don't want to go to bed."

"That's not fair!"

"I had it first!"

"Did too!"

Typical cries from typical kids. They really are cute when they're young, but occasionally, maybe after cleaning up after them for the millionth time, you can't help but think, "When are they going to grow up?"

It's one thing for a kid to act like, well . . . a kid, but it's quite another when that child is in his or her twenties or thirties.

You might think it strange to find this topic in a book such as this, but there are many people in our culture and, sadly, in the church, who, by their actions, simply refuse to grow up. It's great to have fun, it's a blessing to enjoy life, but there comes a time when we all need to accept our responsibilities as adults. And if we are married, now is that time.

The apostle Paul described it this way: "When I was a child, I spoke as a child, I understood as a child, I thought as a child; but when I became a man, I put away childish things" (1 Corinthians 13:11).

Perpetual adolescence is not God's plan for any of us. His plan is for each of us to grow up just as His Son did—not only in physical stature, but to grow in our wisdom and knowledge of God as well (see Luke 2:52).

Yes, foolish children are a source of grief to their parents, and their spouse as well. The Peter Pan principle—refusing to grow up—makes for a tough marriage, but nothing is impossible with God!

> LORD, YOU KNOW ME BETTER THAN I KNOW MYSELF.
> PLEASE SHOW ME IF THERE ARE ANY AREAS IN WHICH
> I NEED TO MATURE, IN WHICH I NEED TO GROW UP.
> THANK YOU FOR YOUR CONTINUED PATIENCE AND
> GRACE.

A true faith in Jesus Christ will not suffer us to be idle . . . It fills the heart, so that it cannot be easy till it is doing something for Jesus Christ.
GEORGE WHITEFIELD

LOVE IN ACTION

1. Go somewhere and be kids together. Build a sandcastle at the beach. Ride your bikes. Head for the park and swing on the swings. Share a single milkshake with two straws. Enjoy!

2. Take a deep breath. Now ask your spouse if there are any areas in your life that you are still a foolish little girl or boy in an adult's body. Then invite your heavenly Father into the conversation.

THE LORD'S DESIGN

And it came to pass on the way, at the encampment,
that the LORD met him and sought to kill him.

EXODUS 4:24

OKAY, MEN, IT'S NOT a problem that arose with the women's lib movement, and unfortunately it's not all that unique in many churches today. The problem: men abdicating their God-given responsibilities—and in Exodus 4 that abdication almost meant death.

God had commanded the men of Israel to be circumcised. This mark on their body would signify their holiness unto God: a nation set apart from the peoples of the world.

Like many of God's commands today, this command was ignored—and this time Moses was guilty! This chosen man of God, selected to lead the Lord's people out of Egyptian captivity and into the Promised Land, chose not to obey God's command to circumcise his son. Moses was the head of the home, yet he would not step up and do the godly duty that the Lord had called him to do.

Thankfully Moses' wife was not about to ignore God's command, and she stepped up. By circumcising their son, Moses' wife saved her husband's life.

Do you ever wonder how Moses felt? Was he humbled, or even humiliated, to watch his wife obey the Lord's commands when he had refused to?

How sad it is when God's appointed leaders fail to obey His clear commands. Husbands: we are called to be the heads of our homes. Let's step up!

> LORD, YOUR DESIGN IS FOR THE MAN TO LEAD THE
> FAMILY. PLEASE FORGIVE ME FOR THE WAYS I AM NOT
> MAKING THAT HAPPEN—AND PLEASE SHOW ME HOW TO
> GET MORE IN LINE WITH YOUR PLAN FOR OUR MARRIAGE
> AND OUR FAMILY.

LOVE IN ACTION

1. Men, in a quiet moment with the Lord, consider the honest answers to these questions: Is your wife pursuing Christ with greater zeal than you are? Are you leading your family in the study of God's Word? In what ways, if any, is your wife being the spiritual leader in the home? Pray about any areas of your spiritual walk that need improving.

2. Ladies, ask your husband to share with you one thing that you could be doing to encourage his spiritual leadership. Then commit to it, give him a big hug, and remember that it's easier for him to lead someone who willingly and joyfully wants to help.

We have need to watch carefully over our own hearts, lest fondness for any relation prevail above our love to God, and take us off from our duty to Him.
MATTHEW HENRY

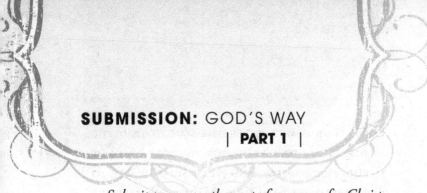

SUBMISSION: GOD'S WAY
| PART 1 |

Submit to one another out of reverence for Christ.

EPHESIANS 5:21 NIV

W AIT A MINUTE . . . If children are supposed to submit to their parents, wives are supposed to submit to their husbands, and workers are supposed to submit to their bosses, how could the apostle Paul tell everyone to "submit to *one another*"?

A misunderstanding of this passage can lead to chaos in all these relationships and more. Here's what we know: the Bible is clear that while we are all one in Christ (Galatians 3:28), God has assigned us different *roles*. In today's verse, Paul addressed the *attitude* that each of us must have as we perform our roles. In other words, all of us are to walk in the Spirit and have a genuine, humble heart toward everyone—no matter our role.

This type of mutual submission means that regardless of our position, we are to have the attitude of consideration toward others. Even if God has placed us in a role of authority (moms to children, pastors to church members, governors to constituents, etc.), we are not to take our God-ordained position as a license to lord it over those whom He has graciously put under our care. Sadly, there are many examples of husbands, teachers, pastors, and pretty much anyone in leadership who have abused their positions and have not been true servant leaders.

Jesus Christ is the supreme example of servant leadership. When He walked this earth, He had supreme authority over sin and demons, as well as the authority to teach both His disciples and the religious leaders of the day. But He never abused those under His authority by treating them as less than who they were—a special creation of God.

As we mutually submit to each other, we find sweetness in our roles, the husband as head of the house and his wife submitting to him. Don't believe it? Hey, get your heart in the right place, rely on the Holy Spirit for help, and give it a shot.

> LORD, HELP US TO HUMBLY SUBMIT TO ONE ANOTHER
> IN THE SAME WAY THAT JESUS HIMSELF DID—FOR OUR
> GOOD AND FOR YOUR GLORY.

The right manner of growth is to grow less in one's own eyes.
THOMAS WATSON

LOVE IN ACTION

1. Talk about how biblical submission can be regarded as an act of love—and why our society doesn't see it that way.

2. Read Ephesians 5:1–21. Discuss with each other negative examples of not walking in the Spirit, as well as positive examples of what happens when we do. Talk about the effects walking in the Spirit can have on your marriage.

SUBMISSION: GOD'S WAY
| PART 2 |

Wives, submit to your husbands as to the Lord. For the husband
is the head of the wife as Christ is the head of the church.

EPHESIANS 5:22 NIV

S UBMIT TO MY HUSBAND? No way, Jose! That barbaric way of life has
been dead since the sixties!

That is often the response of countless women after reading Paul's
command above, but the Bible is never wrong. Beginning with the first
husband and wife, God established the structure of marriage: Adam was
the head of Eve (Genesis 3:16). At that moment, God definitively ordained
our roles within marriage, and these roles, yet another act of His mercy
and grace, are designed to keep order and administer blessing just as He
intended.

Wives are called to submit to their husbands just as they submit to the
Lord. And when wives willingly submit to their husbands, they will experience blessings from our loving God.

Some wives, if they are married to a difficult or a passive man, or if they
tend to be strong willed themselves, will find the role of submission harder
than others, but that does not give them license to disobey the Word.
What helps in these situations is to keep the focus on as obeying the *Lord*,
not man, for "even if any of them [husbands] are disobedient to the word,
they may be won without a word by the behavior of their wives, as they
observe your chaste and respectful behavior . . . [by] the imperishable qual-
ity of [your] gentle and quiet spirit, which is precious in the sight of God"
(1 Peter 3:1–2, 4 NASB).

God designed our roles in marriage the same way He designed everything else—for His glory and for our good. Wives, seek to honor Him with a humble desire to come under your husband just as you come under Christ.

And, men, strive continually to be a man worthy of your wife's respect, love, and submission.

> LORD GOD, IT'S ONE THING TO KNOW WHAT YOU WANT FROM ME; IT'S ANOTHER TO DO IT. PLEASE TEACH US AND TRANSFORM US INTO A WIFE WHO RESPECTFULLY SUBMITS TO HER HUSBAND AND A HUSBAND WHO LOVINGLY FILLS HIS GOD-GIVEN POSITION AS HEAD OF THE HOUSE.

[God] gave the wife unto the husband to be, not his servant, but his helper, counselor, and comforter.

JOHN DOWNAME

LOVE IN ACTION

1. Each of you choose an activity—riding bikes, bowling, swimming, whatever—and just do it! Have fun being together—and, no, ladies, you don't have to let your husband win.

2. Think back, both of you, about any bad associations you have had with the idea of submission. What were the sources? What truth do you now understand that counters those wrong thoughts and negative connotations?

SUBMISSION: GOD'S WAY
| PART 3 |

*Husbands, love your wives, just as Christ loved the church
and gave himself up for her.*

EPHESIANS 5:25 NIV

O KAY, HUSBANDS. BEFORE IT slips off your tongue, before it even crosses your mind, before you are even remotely tempted to think for one second, *Cool. My wife has to submit to me,* please read the above verse. Now read it again. Now say it out loud.

Men, we may have difficult assignments throughout our lives, but is there a more intimidating task than the command to love our wife just as Christ loved the church and gave Himself up for her?

There are seemingly endless implications from this passage, but here are five:

* *Patience.* Christ is patient with us when we sin and fail—and we do so often and repeatedly. Husbands, we are to show Christlike patience, a calm endurance with our wives as God works to grow them.

* *Purification.* Christ purifies our hearts and our minds on a daily basis. We are called to gently lead and encourage our wives toward holiness just as Jesus continually purifies us.

* *Protection.* Christ protects us in so many ways, physically and spiritually. In turn, we are to protect our wives from bad influences, as well as unprofitable relationships or activities.

* *Permanence.* Once we are His, we are always His. Jesus never gives up on us. And just as His love for us is permanent, our love for and commitment to our wives and our marriage are to be permanent.

* *Perfection.* Christ is the only one who accomplished it. Obviously we'll never hit it in this life. But as the spiritual leader in our home, we are to strive with all diligence to be growing, disciplined, Christlike examples to our wives.

So, husbands, before you get too excited about being the leader of your wife, think of the great weight of that responsibility. May we humbly beg the Lord's grace as we seek to love our wives as Christ loved the church.

> SERVANT-LEADERSHIP. I SEE IT MODELED BY YOUR SON, LORD GOD, AND I WANT TO FOLLOW HIS EXAMPLE. PLEASE KEEP MY PRIDE AND SELF-SUFFICIENCY OUT OF THE PICTURE, AND HELP ME BE A GOOD STEWARD OF THE WIFE YOU'VE ENTRUSTED TO MY CARE.

LOVE IN ACTION

1. Wives, tell your husband three ways that he is a good leader of your home. Husbands, tell your wife three areas in which you desire to grow in your servant-leadership. Pray and thank the Lord for His grace.

2. Wrap up this three-day look at submission by making a meal together. Cook, eat, and even clean up together . . . Then praise God for establishing roles within marriage. Then turn off the lights and enjoy dessert.

Unkind and domineering husbands ought not to pretend to be Christians, for they act clean contrary to Christ's demands.
CHARLES SPURGEON

Love Is Patient | *Love suffers long.*
I CORINTHIANS 13:4

"I LOVED THAT MOVIE!" . . . "I love their Caesar salad!" . . . "I love that color on you!" . . . "I love golden retrievers!" . . .

When we use the word *love*—and we tend to use it a lot!—we are often talking about the good feelings we experience as a result of whatever we like or enjoy. The movie left us laughing, crying, thinking, admiring, or at least believing it was worth the ticket price. The Caesar salad makes us feel satisfied. The right shade of blue makes our spouse look dynamite, always a good reflection on us. And there's nothing like a golden retriever's welcome-home wag to warm a heart.

Interestingly, when the apostle Paul described love, he did not refer to the "warm and fuzzy" feelings we *get*, but rather the actions and attitudes we *give*. The apostle began by describing love as "suffers long" (NKJV) or "patient" (NIV). Clearly, Paul's understanding of love went beyond our superficial overuse of the word.

Genuine, Christlike love begins with patience, and we'd all agree that love for our spouse indeed requires patience. Author and theologian Matthew Henry wrote that such longsuffering "will put up with many slights and neglects from the person it loves, and wait long to see the kindly effects of such patience."

Slights and neglects—we've all experienced them, and we're all guilty of them. In every marriage, wrongs are done and injuries experienced, yet God calls us to be longsuffering with our spouse just as Christ is with us. Think of the immeasurable patience Jesus shows us as we stumble along on the path of growing in His grace.

So choose patience. Choose to overlook irritations and offenses. Choose to put longsuffering into action and witness for yourself the lasting "kindly effects" these actions have. You'll find that an extra breath of patience brings calmness to your heart and joy to the soul of your marriage.

> LORD GOD, TEACH ME TO LOVE MY SPOUSE WITH A LOVE THAT IS PATIENT. HELP ME OVERLOOK IRRITATIONS AND OFFENSES. ENABLE ME TO LOVE WITH THE LONGSUFFERING THAT YOU COMMAND AND THAT JESUS HIMSELF EXTENDS TO SINFUL, STUMBLING ME.

LOVE IN ACTION

1. List some ways God has shown patience to you individually and as a couple. Thank Him for His patience and ask Him to help you be patient with each other.

2. Be aware of opportunities to show your spouse patient love. Go shopping with her without a time limit or watch a weekend sporting event with him, regardless of how many projects beckon. Such patient love will transform your marriage.

To lengthen my patience is the best way to shorten my troubles.
GEORGE SWINNOCK

DO UNTO OTHERS

Love...is kind.

I CORINTHIANS 13:4

* She washed his car and even vacuumed it . . .
* He emptied the dishwasher—without being asked . . .
* That favorite meal was just what he needed after a tough day at work . . .
* That backrub made everything right with the world after a crazy day of cleaning, kids, and the everyday chaos of home . . .

CTS OF KINDNESS—OF EXTENDING GOODWILL to others—may happen spontaneously or require some forethought and creativity. They usually don't cost much more than a few minutes and a little energy, and the return on those costs can be amazing! After all, as Paul told us in his description of godly love, love is kind.

The Scriptures teach that, though we are completely unworthy, we believers are recipients of the immeasurable riches of kindness in Jesus Christ—both in this life and for all eternity (Ephesians 2:7). Who are we, then, to *not* extend kindness to our spouse?

We are to show our love for our Lord as well as for our spouse through the acts of kindness we extend to him or her. So why do we oftentimes fail to be kind? To extend acts of goodwill toward them? Is it that we don't want to invest the time and energy? Or that we're too focused on our own needs because we're tired or preoccupied with providing for the family? If we look hard enough, we'll find that the root problem is usually selfishness.

Let's consider the roadblocks to kindness that we encounter in our heart and in everyday life . . . and then confess them and call on the Lord to help us love our spouse with His kind love.

> LORD GOD, GIVE ME EYES TO SEE WHEN AN ACT OF
> KINDNESS CAN BE A MUCH APPRECIATED ACT OF LOVE—
> AND GIVE ME THE HEART TO SERVE MY SPOUSE IN THAT
> WAY.

Do all the good you can, by all the means you can, in all the ways you can, in all the places you can, at all the times you can, to all the people you can, as long as ever you can.
JOHN WESLEY

LOVE IN ACTION

1. "What can I do to help you today?" Try starting the day with that—and then be sure to come through. Just as God's kindness can lead us to repentance (Romans 2:4), our godly kindness to our spouse can lead to greater intimacy and joy in our marriage.

2. Are your eyes open to your spouse's acts of thoughtfulness toward you? A warm hug and a heartfelt "thank you" can fuel the fire of kindness in both of you. Make a conscious effort to acknowledge your spouse's efforts of helpfulness, gentleness, sympathy, and encouragement.

NO ROOM
FOR **ENVY**

Love does not envy.

1 CORINTHIANS 13:4

THE ROOTS OF ENVY—NO pun intended—go back to the Garden.

Eve wanted to be like God: she envied the Almighty's knowledge of good and evil (Genesis 3:4–6). So she ate the fruit, and life on this earth hasn't been the same since. And just as Eve was jealous of God, Cain was jealous of Abel (Genesis 4:5), Joseph's brothers were jealous of him (Genesis 37:4), and Saul was jealous of David (1 Samuel 18:8–9).

So what about us? Jealousy within marriage is not uncommon, so it's important to be honest with ourselves about harboring jealousy toward the very person God blessed us with as a lifetime partner. Is there a pang inside when you think about how she gets to work from home while you're out fighting the elements just to get to the office? Or maybe you envy that everyone is drawn to his vivacious personality while you struggle with shyness?

The opposite of being jealous or envious, then, is rejoicing in what others have; it is rejoicing in the gifts and abilities God has blessed them with. If you're really honest with yourself, your spouse's gifts, abilities, and roles are probably an amazing complement to yours (okay, *most* of them!), giving the two of you a rich and fulfilling union as well as an effective partnership for dealing with life's challenges. And that's a reason to celebrate rather than envy!

> SOVEREIGN LORD, WE ACKNOWLEDGE THAT YOU BROUGHT US TOGETHER. YOUR PLAN CALLS FOR A HUSBAND AND WIFE TO COMPLEMENT AND COMPLETE EACH OTHER, NOT BE CLONES OF EACH OTHER. HELP EACH OF US TO HONESTLY SEARCH OUR HEART FOR ANY AREAS OF JEALOUSY TOWARD THE OTHER. GIVE US THE DESIRE TO REJOICE OVER RATHER THAN ENVY THE GIFTS, ABILITIES, AND OPPORTUNITIES YOU HAVE GIVEN EACH OF US. ENABLE US TO CELEBRATE OUR DIFFERENCES AND TO SEE THEM AS A SOURCE OF STRENGTH FOR BOTH OF US.

All covetousness implies a discontent with our own condition.
THOMAS BOSTON

LOVE IN ACTION

1. Which of your spouse's gifts and abilities have you ever felt envious of, even if just a twinge, even if just for a moment? Or when have you been jealous about your spouse's role—that, for instance, he gets to go to work or she gets to be home with the kids?

2. Look at your answers to the first question. In what ways do you and your spouse complement and complete each other? In what ways is your partnership for life's challenges stronger because of your spouse's talents and personality? Choose thankfulness instead of envy.

LOVE DOES NOT BRAG

Love does not parade itself, is not puffed up.

I CORINTHIANS 13:4

AYBE IT'S BECAUSE OF the big promotion we got at work . . .

Or perhaps because we lost six pounds . . .

Or maybe even because, unlike our spouse, we got up early three straight days and spent time with the Lord . . .

Whatever the accomplishment, there is one temptation we all face: bragging.

Let's face it. God knows us better than we know ourselves, and He sure nailed it when He said in His Word that we all think too highly of ourselves (James 4:1–2, 6). Out of pride we brag. We get puffed up by how great we (want to) think we are. And often our bragging leads to the inevitable: comparing ourselves with others and tearing them down. But such actions are the complete opposite of true and godly love—and unfortunately they can appear in our marriage.

Is she relishing the fact that she earns more than he does?

Does he secretly look at his college degree as proof of his superior intelligence?

Is she secretly glad the kids ignore their father but will do what she wants?

Does he wish she would work out as faithfully as he does so she can look as good?

Parading our abilities, no matter what they are, stems from pride. And being puffed up never helps your relationship, but rather *drains* the nurturing environment needed to grow strong in love with our spouse. Godly love looks up—to our spouse, as well as to God Himself. "Let nothing be done through selfish ambition or conceit, but in lowliness of mind let each esteem others better than himself" (Philippians 2:3). Building up our spouse means less of us, more of them, and ultimately more of Him!

> LORD GOD, KEEP MY EYES FOCUSED ON THE CROSS OF JESUS AND THE PICTURE IT OFFERS OF YOUR LOVE FOR ME. MAY I BE SO HUMBLED BY YOUR LOVE THAT I CAN BUILD UP MY SPOUSE RATHER THAN TEAR HIM OR HER DOWN. HOLY SPIRIT, CONVICT ME BEFORE I SPEAK SO THAT MY WORDS UPLIFT YOU AND YOUR GLORY IN EVERY ASPECT OF MY MARRIAGE.

Pride loves to climb up, not as Zacchaeus to see Christ, but to be seen.
WILLIAM GURNALL

LOVE IN ACTION

1. Think back over the past few days or so. Are there any puffed up words and/or attitudes for which you need to ask God's forgiveness—and your spouse's? Take a few moments to do so now.

2. Okay, maybe it's corny, but write your spouse's name vertically on a piece of paper. Then, at every letter, note something you love about them, whether an accomplishment, skill, or a godly trait that you admire. When you're finished, give the paper to your spouse and thank them for being, well . . . *them!* And thank God for His grace in giving you your precious mate!

A GOLDEN (RULE) OPPORTUNITY

Love . . . does not behave rudely.

I CORINTHIANS 13:4–5

HOME IS WHERE WE let our hair down. We relax and unwind; we freely share our opinions and vent our frustrations. Home is where he doesn't have to shave, and she doesn't have to put on mascara—it's where we can transparently be ourselves. And all that's well and good. But . . .

Letting our hair down does not mean letting basic courtesies go by the wayside. Interrupting when someone is talking; turning the TV volume too loud when someone is trying to take a nap; making jokes or being sarcastic at another's expense—we all can be inconsiderate at times. But, as the apostle Paul put it, love is not rude.

Our sense of entitlement or our sinful self-centeredness is often behind our rudeness, but as we seek to honor God with a lifestyle of gracious, thoughtful, and respectful interactions with our spouse, home will be a much more pleasant place.

Now be honest with yourself. What rude words or actions have you been guilty of in the recent past? It's probably easier to identify such missteps in your spouse, but you're the only one you can change. Ask forgiveness for any offense that resulted and do what you can to make up for any ill feelings. Let basic politeness oil the wheels of your day-to-day married life.

FATHER GOD, YOU KNOW THAT RUDENESS AND
ARROGANCE COME MORE NATURALLY AND EASILY TO
ME THAN KINDNESS AND POLITENESS. I YIELD TO
YOUR SPIRIT NOW AND ASK YOU TO TRANSFORM ME,
CHANGE ME, SO THAT YOUR LOVE WILL OVERPOWER
MY SINFUL NATURE—FOR YOUR GLORY AND THE
GOOD OF MY MARRIAGE.

LOVE IN ACTION

1. Let your spouse be a mirror of how you act around the house. Ask him or her this question—and don't shoot the messenger when you hear the answer! Take a deep breath and then ask, "What rude behaviors am I guilty of?" Thank your spouse for the honest answer and ask them to please pray for you as you work on doing better.

2. Come up with special and significant ways to show respect and courtesy to your spouse for all that he or she does and is for you. Then do them! We all want to be appreciated.

How gentle and tender ought we to be with others who are foolish when we remember how foolish we are, ourselves!
CHARLES
SPURGEON

MY WAY, YOUR WAY, OR OUR WAY?

Love . . . does not seek its own.

I CORINTHIANS 13:4–5

IT WAS A WISE friend who told the new mom, "Parenting is an exercise in dying to self." Well, the same can be said about marriage.

* It bothers you that I want to spend time with my friends?
* I've always opened presents on Christmas morning, not Christmas Eve.
* I told you, when I get home from work I don't like talking about my day.
* I hate sleeping in air-conditioned air—even if it's a thousand degrees outside.

You can undoubtedly add to the list of opportunities you've had to die to yourself—to your habits, your preferences, your way of doing things—since you said, "I do." And that's what love is all about. It's caring about the other person. Love is living out the truth that life is not all about me! Love is not self-centered; love "does not seek its own."

Instead, Christlike love seeks to serve: Jesus Himself "made Himself of no reputation, taking the form of a bond servant . . . He humbled Himself and became obedient to the point of death, even the death of the cross" (Philippians 2:7–8). We die to our natural and sinful self-centeredness when, in the course of daily life, we look for ways to serve our spouse by tending to his or her needs, desires, and preferences before tending to our own.

LORD GOD, THIS IS NOT AN EASY ASSIGNMENT! BUT I KNOW IT'S NOT ALWAYS EASY TO DO WHAT'S RIGHT. SO PLEASE HELP ME DIE TO MY SELF-CENTEREDNESS. GROW IN MY HEART THE DESIRE TO SERVE MY SPOUSE AND, BY SO DOING, TO SERVE AND GLORIFY YOU.

> *He is no Christian who does not seek to serve his God. The very motto of the Christian should be "I serve."*
> CHARLES SPURGEON

LOVE IN ACTION

1. Most married couples fall into patterns: his chores and hers. Serve your spouse this week by doing something on their unwritten list of household chores.

2. Dying to self and serving one's spouse doesn't always mean doing *for*. It can also mean doing *without*. What is one thing—one activity or preference or way of doing things—that you will forgo this week as an act of love for your spouse? And just a thought: don't nominate yourself for sainthood when you do. The effect won't be the same.

Love's Long Fuse | *Love . . . is not provoked.*

I CORINTHIANS 13:4–5

A SHORT FUSE AND godly love are like oil and water: they just don't mix!

Think about Jesus' life and how patient He was with clueless disciples and hypocritical priests. Remember how He welcomed children (Matthew 19:14), tax collectors (Mark 2:15), and even prostitutes (Luke 7:36–50) into His presence. Reflect on His exchange with the criminal crucified with Him on Golgotha (Luke 23:43) or, after His resurrection, with the doubting disciple Thomas (John 20:29). Jesus, our sinless example of righteousness, was definitely not "easily angered" (NIV).

What about you? What would the peanut gallery at home, the folks at the office, the parents of the kids you coach, or (most important) the person who knows you best—your spouse—say about how long your fuse is?

You've undoubtedly heard the bit of wisdom "Count to ten before you speak" if you are angry. Take that suggestion one better and use that counting time to pray and ask God to help you control your anger. Memorize and quote a Scripture verse such as, "Set a guard, O LORD, over my mouth; keep watch over the door of my lips" (Psalm 141:3). As you get into the pattern of turning to Him before you explode, you just may find your fuse growing longer.

LORD GOD, WHY IS IT THAT I CAN BE FAR MORE PATIENT—LESS EASILY PROVOKED—WITH MY FRIENDS THAN WITH MY SPOUSE? WHY AM I MORE PATIENT AT THE OFFICE, IN THE NEIGHBORHOOD, OR EVEN WITH THE LITTLE LEAGUE TEAM, BROWNIE TROOP, OR SUNDAY SCHOOL CLASS THAN I AM WITH MY OWN SPOUSE? PLEASE, LORD, WORK IN ME. PLEASE HELP ME BECOME LESS EASILY ANGERED, BECAUSE THEN MY LOVE FOR MY SPOUSE WILL BE MORE LIKE YOUR LOVE FOR ME.

LOVE IN ACTION

1. Think over the past week. What contributed to those times—especially at home—when you were most easily angered? What can you do to defuse the time bomb inside of you so that you're not about to explode?

2. Talk with your spouse about a good strategy for dealing with each other's short fuse and/or for helping your spouse's fuse grow. Of course you can invite the Lord into the conversation.

He that will be angry, and not sin, must not be angry but for sin.
JOHN TRAPP

NO SCORECARD NEEDED

Love . . . thinks no evil.

1 CORINTHIANS 13:4–5

I'T'S A BIT OF advice most married couples have been told at some point: when there's a disagreement, stay focused on the matter at hand.

Here's an example of what not to do:

Her: Of course I'm upset! You said you'd be home by 6:00. I have dinner ready. Then you call me at 7:00 to say you're on your way!

Him: What can I say? The meeting ran late.

Her: The meeting ran late . . . just like last summer when you said you'd fix the sprinklers.

Him: I thought we were past that.

Her: Or when you said you'd hang the curtains by Thanksgiving . . .

In this example the wife doesn't stay focused, but it can easily happen to either spouse. Someone is keeping score and, in a moment of frustration, the "record of wrongs" is dragged out. All this ammunition, being fired all at once, does nothing to foster feelings of love!

A better and biblical strategy is to not store up that collection of wrongs and offenses. When we have sinned against each other and have asked forgiveness, our sin is to be wiped out for good. We are not to drag up old things from the past in order to use them in the present against our spouse. God "blots out your transgressions . . . [and] will not remember your sins" (Isaiah 43:25). We are to extend the same grace to each other.

> LORD, IT'S HARD TO LET GO OF THOSE WRONGS DONE
> AGAINST ME, THOSE HURTS I'VE EXPERIENCED IN MY
> MARRIAGE, AND THE CONSEQUENCES OF MY SPOUSE'S SIN
> THAT HAVE IMPACTED ME. PLEASE HELP ME FORGIVE . . .
> AND LET GO OF MY LIST ONCE AND FOR ALL.

Our forgiving of others will not procure forgiveness for ourselves; but our not forgiving others proves that we ourselves are not forgiven.
JOHN OWEN

LOVE IN ACTION

1. If you happen to have a mental record of your spouse's wrongdoings toward you, it's time to get rid of that list. Write down the list of your spouse's offenses—and then burn that paper.

2. Talk together about how you both can process hurts, sins, or wrongdoings to help you avoid keeping score or making that mental list. Then you can focus on the issue at hand and not try to defend yourself for or against what happened long ago.

NO **TOLERANCE**

Love . . . does not rejoice in iniquity.

I CORINTHIANS 13:4, 6

HOW COULD LIGHT CELEBRATE darkness? How could a holy God rejoice in unholiness?

The truth is . . . light cannot celebrate darkness, and our holy God does not tolerate unholiness. Likewise, we are called to "not rejoice in iniquity." God hates sin, and when we don't gently confront another's sin, we show a lack of love, not just for that person, but for God.

In sharp contrast to being blind to or silent about sin, we are to rejoice in a purity of heart and in a life of holiness. "The precepts of the LORD are right, rejoicing the heart; The commandment of the LORD is pure, enlightening the eyes" (Psalm 19:8 NASB). We are to encourage our spouse to put out of his or her life those activities that indicate an acceptance of sin—like watching television programs and movies that glorify sin or frequenting places where sin is apparently the norm. Isaiah said, "Woe to those who call evil good, and good evil" (Isaiah 5:20). May we not be found among those!

LORD GOD, IT IS ALL TOO EASY TO TOLERATE THE SIN IN OUR SOCIETY, SIN THAT HAS BECOME THE NORM—AND IT IS ALL TOO EASY TO TOLERATE SIN IN OURSELVES. BUT YOU CALL US TO A HIGHER STANDARD. PLEASE WORK IN OUR HEARTS SO THAT WE GRIEVE OVER SIN AS YOU DO. PURIFY OUR HEARTS SO THAT WE CAN EXPERIENCE THE REJOICING THAT YOU HAVE PROMISED, LEADING TO PURE AND GODLY LIVING THAT HONORS YOU.

If once you know it to be a sin, you need not reason the condition of admission or not, or what will follow. You immediately reject it without deliberation. Because there is no good in it.
JEREMIAH
BURROUGHS

LOVE IN ACTION

1. Our requests of others carry more weight if we ourselves are doing what we are asking them to do. So take a few minutes and ask God to show you behaviors that indicate your tolerance of sin. It may be enjoying coarse jokes received online or perhaps heart issues, like carrying grudges. Then, rather than merely talking about making these changes for good or right, do it!

2. If you need to confront your spouse about an area of sin, be sure to deal with the log in your own eye first. Spend some time in prayer and let God show you your sin. Confess and repent of it. Ask His guidance for how to approach your spouse, and remember . . . your part is to expose the truth in love. It's God's job to change a person's heart.

LOVE
AND TRUTH

Love . . . rejoices in the truth.

I CORINTHIANS 13:6

W HAT COMES TO MIND when you hear the word *truth*? Not lying? Not hiding what you're feeling or shading what you're thinking? The reality that Jesus died on the cross for our sin and rose from the dead on the third day? The truth referred to in 1 Corinthians 13:6 is all this and more.

Godly love rejoices in the telling of the truth even if the truth requires painful self-evaluation and difficult steps of repentance. Godly love also values an accurate, truthful portrayal of oneself: Jesus condemns hypocrisy. And godly love rejoices in the truth found in God's Word. Compromising on, rather than obeying, the commands of God's true Word for your life and your marriage is to not love at all.

In other words, God's truth—His commands, His exhortations, the example of His Son's sacrificial and servant love—is to inform our daily life and our marriage. When we spend time studying His Word, individually and especially together, we will grow to love each other more. It's that simple, and . . . it's true! Give it a try and see!

In our postmodern, relativistic world, Lord God, truth is not valued the way You value it. We human beings like to live life our way and then justify it with a version of truth all our own. Show me where I am doing that—and help my marriage to be informed and transformed by Your gospel truth and its ability to guide and empower.

LOVE IN ACTION

1. "Apart from the truth of God's Word, there is no real love." Talk about this statement, wrestle with what it means, and decide whether you and your spouse agree or disagree.

2. It's time for a Bible treasure hunt! Look up these three gems: 1 Peter 2:1–2, Joshua 1:8 and Psalm 1:1–2. Say them aloud and thank Him for His life-giving, life-changing truth. (For extra credit, commit these three treasures to memory!)

The word of God should not only be in the Bible, but the Bible should be in a man's life. A man's life should be a walking Bible.
WILLIAM FENNER

THERE'S NO FINE PRINT

Love . . . bears all things.

I CORINTHIANS 13:4, 7

WHAT COMES TO MIND when you hear the phrase "love . . . bears all things"?

* Perhaps you think of dealing with his insistence that hot sauce goes on everything . . . or with her borderline OCD concern that the cap is on the toothpaste tube and that all the paste is pushed toward the opening.
* Or you cringe inside when you hear your spouse tell the same old jokes over, and over . . . and over—but you force a smile.
* Maybe, in spite your disdain for long road trips, you still pack the van for the traditional holiday visit to the in-laws.

Love bears *all* these things—and infinitely more. Godly love also bears a spouse's imperfections and sin. Of course we don't overlook that sin, but we also don't broadcast the issue. We keep private, within the safe confines of the marriage bond, the sin our spouse is struggling to get free of. We pray, we listen, we support, we hold accountable, we do whatever he or she needs us to do during the battle.

Our spouse's sin can wound us just as ours can wound him or her, but we aren't to add greater hurt by telling people about the struggle. There may be situations where seeking the counsel of a pastor or godly friend is wise, but the point here is that we don't gossip or unnecessarily let others know about this private matter.

LORD, YOU'RE HOLDING ME TO MY MARRIAGE VOWS, AND THAT'S HOW IT SHOULD BE. JUST AS JESUS PERSEVERED WITH THE HARD-TO-LOVE SINNERS IN HIS INNER CIRCLE, HELP ME TO BEAR MY SPOUSE'S BURDENS AND GENTLY ENCOURAGE HIM OR HER TOWARD CHRISTLIKENESS IN EVERY WAY. AND HELP ME TO REMEMBER THAT HE OR SHE IS BEARING ALL THINGS OF MINE AT THE SAME TIME!

LOVE IN ACTION

1. Be honest. In living with you, what "bears all things" matters is your spouse dealing with? List the top five of your issues, imperfections, idiosyncrasies, and sin—the "worse" of "for better or worse"—that he or she vowed to bear. Let this humbling perspective on yourself prompt you to be more patient with your spouse—who, living with you, doesn't have it all that easy either!

2. Talk together about how to best support each other during life's current struggles. Yes, life is difficult, but having the hope of the gospel sure makes it easier to keep pressing on in your relationship.

Love covers unworthy things rather than bringing them to the light and magnifying them. It puts up with everything. It is always eager to believe the best and to "put the most favorable construction on ambiguous actions."
ALBERT BARNES

JUMPING TO CONCLUSIONS

Love . . . believes all things.

I CORINTHIANS 13:7

"I can't believe she did that! What was she thinking?!"

Maybe she really did have your best interest in mind . . .

"Did he do that just to make me angry? If that was his goal, he nailed it!"

Maybe that wasn't his goal . . .

JUMPING TO CONCLUSIONS ABOUT our spouse's motive in a given situation is always a bad idea—and yet we can do exactly that in a fraction of a second! And whenever we take that kind of mental misstep, we put our spouse on the defensive and usually end up eating our words and regretting our actions later.

Another very important aspect of loving our spouse is choosing to believe the best about them until proven otherwise. To love our spouse is to believe that she has the best of intentions in all that she does; it is to give him the benefit of the doubt, especially when it's not obvious what he is doing or why.

May our belief in the Lord—in His sovereign power, His good plans for us, His commitment to the institution of marriage—remind us that He can and does bring beauty out of ashes, that nothing is impossible for Him, and that nothing can separate us from His redemptive, healing, transforming love. If that belief is unshakable, we will better weather the tough times in our marriage. God is on your side! Believe it!

Believe in the good intentions of your spouse and the faithfulness of your God . . . always.

"I BELIEVE; HELP MY UNBELIEF" (MARK 9:24).
I'M SO GLAD YOU HONOR THAT PRAYER—AND I'M
GRATEFUL, LORD, THAT YOU NEVER LET GO OF US.
YOU CAN HELP UNTANGLE THE MISUNDERSTOOD
MOTIVES AND UNINTENDED CONSEQUENCES OF OUR
ACTIONS. YOU CAN DO THE SEEMINGLY IMPOSSIBLE
IN OUR MARRIAGE, IN OUR LIFE CIRCUMSTANCES,
AND IN OUR HEART. MAY WE BUILD OUR MARRIAGE
AND OUR LIVES ON THIS TRUTH.

We ought to be very candid in our censures of others, because we need grains of allowance ourselves.
MATTHEW HENRY

LOVE IN ACTION

1. Humor may help drive this point home. Think back on a time when you jumped to conclusions about a person's motive and then realized you were totally wrong. Or maybe you and your motives have been misunderstood. What happened when the two of you realized what the other was thinking?

2. What can you do to foster the tendency to believe the best of each other? To reinforce your faith in God and the truth that He is on your side, tell three or four "faith stories"—accounts of when God clearly intervened on your behalf.

NEVER SAY "NEVER"

Love . . . hopes all things.

I CORINTHIANS 13:4, 7

* "He'll never stop putting work ahead of our marriage, and I'm just plain tired of it."
* "She'll never understand how her negative words and attitudes impact me. It's hard to not give up on this relationship."
* "He'll never stop bringing up the past, so what's the use of trying anymore?"

MARRIAGE IS HARD WORK, and when the road has been rough for too long, feelings of hopelessness can take up residency in hearts and minds. That's when we need to turn to the Lord with renewed commitment to let His love transform our love—our hearts and our minds—for each other. *Only* in Him can we find hope when our relationship seems hopeless.

Godly love doesn't say, "He'll never change." Godly love looks first to the Lord of hope and then to oneself or one's spouse and proclaims, "I have hope that the resurrection power of God can transform our hearts, our behavior, and this relationship!"

With our eyes on the Lord and our hope resting in Him, we can encourage our spouse with hope for the future, with hope for renewal and redemption. Ideally, our spouse will be able to offer us the same hope-based encouragement when we need it.

Waiting patiently for God to act in a given situation and with a worn-out heart is not an easy assignment, but choose to remember that God is doing His transforming work even as we wait prayerfully on Him.

HELP ME, LORD, TO "HOLD FAST THE CONFESSION OF OUR HOPE WITHOUT WAVERING, FOR [YOU] WHO PROMISED [ARE] FAITHFUL" (HEBREWS 10:23). KEEP MY EYES FOCUSED ON YOU INSTEAD OF ON CIRCUMSTANCES. KEEP MY MIND ROOTED IN YOUR TRUTH AND CONFIDENT IN THE HOPE THAT YOU ARE AT WORK IN OUR HEARTS AND OUR MARRIAGE FOR YOUR GLORY AND OUR GOOD.

> *Hope is never ill when faith is well.*
> JOHN BUNYAN

LOVE IN ACTION

1. Tell an encouraging story about a person that you know or know of whom you have seen completely transformed by God's power and grace. What marriage relationship seemed hopeless but, again by God's power and grace, is now flourishing? Be encouraged by your heavenly Father's unlimited power to restore, redeem, and rebuild.

2. What aspect of life does your spouse especially need to be encouraged about right now? Think of the current challenges and ask God to show you how best to offer encouragement—and then do it.

THE LONG HAUL

Love . . . endures all things.

1 CORINTHIANS 13:4, 7

* Having a sense of humor . . .
* Saying "I love you" regularly . . .
* Kissing each other goodnight . . .
* Not going to bed angry . . .
* Being willing to compromise . . .

ACCORDING TO COUPLES WHO have been married fifty years or longer, these are some of the key reasons they made it that far. But the key factor to the longevity of many marriages is God—and God alone.

To have a marriage anchored in God means we love each other according to Jesus' definition of love. And the final aspect of love from this pinnacle chapter of 1 Corinthians is fitting: love endures all things.

As we journey through life with our spouse, there will certainly be struggles, disappointments, and challenges. When things get tough, we may be tempted to throw in the towel, but that is not the answer for Christians—or for anyone.

Instead, the Scriptures tell us that in those dark times we should, "consider Him who endured such hostility from sinners against Himself, lest [we] become weary and discouraged" (Hebrews 12:3).

It sure is easy to become weary and discouraged, but, as always, Jesus is our model. He experienced pain, suffering, and wrongs done against Him in ways we cannot imagine. Yet He endured it all, including death on the cross.

As we look to Jesus and His example, let us be encouraged that as He grows us to be more and more like Him, we can endure, and we can have hope even in the hard times.

Let's stay committed to the vows we made and to loving our spouse God's way. And when we hit those bumps in the road, let's endure.

> LORD GOD, THERE'S NO FINE PRINT OR EXCLUSIONS HERE. YOU CALL US TO A LOVE THAT "ENDURES ALL THINGS," AND WE CAN ONLY DO THAT IN YOUR STRENGTH. PLEASE HELP US KNOW HOW TO KEEP OUR MARRIAGE STRONG AND ROOTED IN YOU SO, TO YOUR GLORY, WE ENDURE FOR THE LONG HAUL.

LOVE IN ACTION

1. What are you doing—or could you be doing—to keep your love for each other rooted in your love for God and His love for you?

2. In the privacy of your own home, encourage each other by reaffirming your wedding vows. Make up new ones if you have to, but make sure to include "til death do us part."

Our motto must continue to be perseverance. And ultimately I trust the Almighty will crown our efforts with success.
WILLIAM WILBERFORCE

ALIEN RIGHTEOUSNESS—AND MARRIAGE

For He made Him who knew no sin to be sin for us,
that we might become the righteousness of God in Him.

2 CORINTHIANS 5:21

HERE YOU GO! BASIC Doctrine 101. It's good stuff—and critical to a Christian marriage. If you doubt that, keep reading.

Jesus came to earth to redeem those whom God the Father had chosen to be His before the foundation of the world. The perfect God-Man, Jesus was born without sin and He lived free of sin. He obeyed God's laws perfectly, yet He died in the place of sinners as if He were a sinner Himself (1 Corinthians 15:3).

Sin is an offense to the Lord's holiness, and the Bible is clear that the wages, or payment, for our sin is death (Romans 6:23). God demands a perfect obedience to His law if we are to be declared righteous. When we put our faith in Christ, Jesus' death on the cross *is* that payment for our sin, and Jesus' perfect obedience is credited to our account as if *we* lived a perfectly obedient life. Our alien righteousness (meaning "coming from outside of ourselves") is the righteousness of Jesus Himself. What amazing and humbling grace!

Why is this foundational doctrine critical to a Christian marriage? Because it presents your spouse in a very special light. It confirms that God loves your spouse enough to send His only Son to die on the cross as payment for his or her sin. They are immeasurably precious in the eyes of the Creator. So, are you treating them as such?

> THANK YOU FOR THIS REMINDER OF WHOM I
> MARRIED . . . ONE OF YOUR PRECIOUS CHILDREN,
> FOR WHOM YOUR SON SUFFERED AND DIED AND
> WHO WILL ONE DAY BE RAISED AND GLORIFIED
> WITH YOU. HELP ME TO TREAT MY SPOUSE WITH
> THE HONOR HE OR SHE DESERVE BECAUSE, IF FOR
> NO OTHER REASON, MY SPOUSE IS YOURS. AND HELP
> ME TO WALK HUMBLY WITH YOU IN LIGHT OF THE
> PRICE YOU PAID FOR MY SALVATION.

*He hideth our
unrighteousness
with His
righteousness,
He covereth our
disobedience with
His obedience,
He shadoweth
our death with
His death, that
the wrath of God
cannot find us.*
HENRY SMITH

LOVE IN ACTION

1. Time for an oral exam. When was the last time you heard your spouse's testimony? You each get five minutes to tell each other how you came to understand the truth of the gospel and how the Lord brought you to Himself. Then slow dance together—with or without music.

2. Now that you've had a refresher course on each other's testimonies. Each of you write a one-page letter—maybe to your kids or to a friend or family member—on how the Lord raised your spouse to saving faith in Him.

LOVE ABOUNDING

This I pray, that your love may abound still more and more in knowledge and all discernment.

PHILIPPIANS 1:9

CAUSE AND EFFECT. WE see it all around us.

* We water seeds . . . and they grow.
* We drop something . . . and it breaks.
* We work out without warming up or warming down . . . and we're sore the next day.
* We practice . . . and we become more skilled.

In Philippians 1:9, Paul mentioned both cause (his prayers) and the desired effect ("that your love may abound still more and more"). But notice that Paul didn't stop there. He went on to tell us how we can help our love grow: knowledge and discernment are key.

If we truly want to demonstrate God's love, and if we want our ability to love to abound still more, we begin by re-dedicating ourselves to the study of His Word because that is where we find true knowledge and discernment.

As we learn more of who God is and what He commands, and as we respond to those commands in obedience, we will find ourselves—by God's grace and His Spirit's transforming power—growing in our love for others. And, yes, that "others" includes our spouse.

> LORD, WE REALIZE THAT WE NEED A GROWING KNOWLEDGE OF YOU
> IF WE ARE TO LOVE EACH OTHER IN A WAY THAT PLEASES YOU. OUR
> SPIRITS ARE WILLING TO TRY, BUT ALL TOO OFTEN OUR FLESH IS VERY
> WEAK. PLEASE FUEL OUR LOVE FOR YOU AND EMPOWER OUR LOVE
> FOR EACH OTHER TO ABOUND STILL MORE AND MORE.

LOVE IN ACTION

1. Think of a time in your marriage when God enabled you to love your spouse in a far warmer and more genuine way than you could ever have done on your own. Why was your spouse difficult to love at that time? What made you remember to call on the Lord for His help? Ask God to help you do so again, until it becomes the rule rather than the exception.

2. As we learn more and more of who God is and what He commands, and as we act on that knowledge and in obedience to those commands, we will find ourselves—by God's grace and His Spirit's transforming power—growing in our love for others. List three specific ways you—as a couple—can learn more about God. Commit to putting at least one idea into practice within a week. Then tell each other how much you love them.

The end of all learning is to know God, and out of that knowledge to love and imitate Him.
JOHN MILTON

LOVE
AND HONOR

Be kindly affectionate to one another with brotherly love,
in honor giving preference to one another.

ROMANS 12:10

* It's not my favorite, but she loves that Italian restaurant.
* I like flavored, but I know he likes regular coffee.

ET'S FACE IT, WE all have preferences, and left to ourselves we'd probably rather do things our way—all the time. But as God has made
us a new creation in Christ, it's time to wake up and smell the coffee
(whether flavored or not) and remember it's no longer about us.

In this passage we learn two simple principles that, when put into practice,
can transform our relationships with other believers:

1. We should have a warm family affection toward each other.
2. We should honor our fellow Christians by putting their preferences
   above our own.

Like so many aspects of our walk with God, putting these principles into
practice requires humility.

With humble hearts, we should interact with our brothers and sisters in
Christ as one loving, caring family. And as opportunities arise, we should seek
to honor our family members above ourselves.

As we continue to grow in our ability to live out these truths, we will see
our friendships growing deeper and our fellowship, sweeter.

So the next time you are with a fellow member of the body of Christ, honor
this "sibling" by putting his or her preferences above your own. And who on
the planet should we more quickly yield our preferences to than our spouse?

> LORD, LET ME NEVER FORGET THAT MY SPOUSE IS MY
> SIBLING IN THE LORD. HELP ME TO HONOR MY SPOUSE
> BY PUTTING HIS OR HER PREFERENCES ABOVE MY OWN.
> AND PLEASE LET THIS HUMILITY EXTEND TO ALL MY
> FAMILY IN CHRIST.

I am persuaded that love and humility are the highest attainments in the school of Christ and the brightest evidences that He is indeed our Master.

JOHN NEWTON

LOVE IN ACTION

1. Husbands, in what ways does your wife honor you by putting your preferences above her own? Encourage her by letting her know.

2. Wives, in what ways does your husband honor you by putting your preferences above his own? Encourage him by letting him know. Consider taking an inventory like this on a regular basis.

YOU CAN'T READ MY MIND?

There is an appointed time for everything....
A time to be silent and a time to speak.

ECCLESIASTES 3:1, 7 NASB

O UR TONGUES CAN SURE get us into trouble. More often than not we probably need to heed the wisdom of Solomon and remember there is "a time to be silent."

Equally true, however, we must remember in marriage there is also "a time to speak."

* "Why didn't you say that you weren't in the mood for Mexican when I asked you where you wanted to go for dinner?"
* "If you had a specific idea for celebrating our anniversary, why didn't you let me know when you asked me to get a sitter?"
* "I've been making you pb&j sandwiches with too much jelly for how many years?!?"
* "I never knew you felt so strongly about the time I spend with my friends."

And an appropriate response to each of these four statements might be, "Sorry, I can't read your mind!"

It goes without saying that open and honest communication is critical for a healthy marriage—and we don't want to presume that our spouse always knows what we are thinking or how we are feeling. We must continually cultivate safe and open lines of communication and when it is "time to speak," speak the truth in gentleness and love.

> FATHER GOD, YOU INTEND MARRIAGE TO BE A SAFE PLACE
> FOR BOTH OF US. SAFE TO COMMUNICATE WHAT WE WANT
> WITHOUT FEAR OF CONDEMNATION OR OPPOSITION. PLEASE
> HELP EACH OF US TO BE SENSITIVE TO EACH OTHER'S WANTS
> AND DESIRES. PROMPT US TO LOVE EACH OTHER WITH THE
> SAME LOVE AND CONSIDERATION YOU SHOW US SO THAT OUR
> MARRIAGE CAN BE A SAFE HAVEN FOR TRUTH-SPEAKING.

In our manner of speech, our plans of living, our dealings with others, our conduct and walk in the church and out of it—all should be done as becomes the Gospel.

ALBERT BARNES

LOVE IN ACTION

1. Do you struggle to speak up about your preference or opinion? If so why? With gentleness and love take turns giving an honest assessment as to how well you think your spouse communicates with you.

2. What topics of conversation are stressful for each of you to talk about? Allow each other the freedom to say what they are (even if it's just one at a time) and pray together for God's guidance, wisdom, and love to help you, in time, work together toward a peaceful resolve.

GETTING BACK
ON TRACK **AFTER A FIGHT**

Blessed are the peacemakers.

MATTHEW 5:9

I F YOU'VE BEEN MARRIED for more than a week or two, chances are about 100 percent that you and your spouse have had a fight.

Some fights result from disagreements over life-changing issues, but most fights are usually prompted by little irritants. And often the fight itself is far worse than the original offense that caused the fight in the first place! You know the drill . . .

The transgression occurs ("Can't he put the dirty glass in the dishwasher instead of the sink?" or "She never moves the seat back after she has driven my car"), anger flashes, harsh words are spoken ("You never listen to me!" or "What do you do around here all day anyway?"), feelings are hurt, and you find yourself smothering in the ashy aftermath of the emotional explosion. Your eyes burn, it's hard to breathe, and you wonder how you, as a couple, will find your way to clear blue skies.

Jesus said, "Blessed are the peacemakers." In this post-volcano scenario, being a peacemaker begins with asking for forgiveness—if not for the transgression, then for the overreaction. And seeking forgiveness doesn't need to be prefaced by or followed up with rationale or excuses or even an explanation—only humility.

Humbling yourself is the first step toward making peace. That's not easy to do, but as you practice being a peacemaker, you will see that you are opening the door wider for loving actions to follow.

> LORD GOD, PLEASE HELP US BOTH TO BE LESS
> IRRITATING AND LESS IRRITABLE. TEACH US TO EXTEND
> MORE GRACE TO EACH OTHER INSTEAD OF REACTING
> ANGRILY TO LITTLE IRRITANTS. WHEN WE DO DISAGREE
> OVER A SIGNIFICANT MATTER, PLEASE REMIND US THAT
> WE ARE ON THE SAME TEAM AND THAT YOU ARE WITH
> US. AND, LORD, WHEN WE DO FIGHT, WE ASK THAT YOU
> FREE US FROM PRIDE SO THAT WE CAN HUMBLY SEEK
> EACH OTHER'S FORGIVENESS. WE ASK THESE THINGS
> FOR YOUR GLORY AND OUR GOOD. IN JESUS' NAME.
> AMEN.

LOVE IN ACTION

1. Take a deep breath and ask your spouse, "What is one thing I do that irritates you— just one!—that I can work on stopping? Yes, just one!" And then work on stopping it.

2. Write down three things you appreciate about your spouse and pray for him or her. And it sure wouldn't hurt to share— out loud, in writing, with flowers or brownies—those three affirmations!

When a man's ways please God, the stones of the street shall be at peace with him.
THOMAS WATSON

NEW EVERY MORNING

Through the LORD'S mercies we are not consumed,
Because His compassions fail not.
They are new every morning;
Great is Your faithfulness.

LAMENTATIONS 3:22–23

THE SUN IS PEEKING over the horizon.

The day's paper is hot off the press.

The coffee is freshly brewed.

The morning means a new beginning, and the most important aspect of that new start is the presence of the Lord in our day.

Jeremiah's words of praise tell us that God's mercies and compassion mean a fresh start for us as the sun comes up—they are new every morning.

What does that fresh start look like in your marriage? It could mean that today's the day . . .

* You surprise your spouse with a favorite something . . .
* You spend some time praying for him or her and your relationship . . .
* You write a love note, listing those traits you especially admire and appreciate . . .
* You read God's Word and perhaps find a passage to share with your spouse . . .
* You pray with your spouse before you head in your different directions . . .
* You ask forgiveness for yesterday's selfishness or misspoken words . . .
* You find ten reasons to thank God for your spouse . . .

We start each new day not knowing what will unfold, but knowing that the Lord is full of grace, mercy, and compassion gives enough reason to rejoice and be glad. Extend some of that to your spouse today!

> LORD, THERE IS SOMETHING UNIQUE AND WONDERFUL ABOUT THE ENERGY AND ANTICIPATION THAT COMES WITH THE DAWNING OF A NEW DAY. THANK YOU FOR REMINDING ME TODAY THAT EVERY DAY CAN BE THE DAWNING OF A NEW DAY IN MY MARRIAGE . . . AND THAT YOU WILL BLESS THE TIME AND EFFORT I INVEST IN THIS SACRED RELATIONSHIP WITH MY SPOUSE.

These rivers of mercy run fully and constantly, but never run dry. No; they are new every morning; every morning we have fresh instances of God's compassion towards us.
MATTHEW HENRY

LOVE IN ACTION

1. Talk with your spouse and schedule a time to go out for breakfast or take an early morning walk together. There really is something special about the quiet before the day unfolds.

2. Which of the seven suggestions in today's devotional will you do? Note how it impacts your day and/or your marriage for the better.

SING, SING, SING!

Sing praise to the LORD, you saints of His,
And give thanks at the remembrance of His holy name.

PSALM 30:4

EVER HAVE ONE OF those days when you take a step back and think, "Wow! God sure is good!" Do you ever just feel like singing praises to your heavenly Father at the top of your lungs? (Please, with respect to your spouse, if you can't carry a tune, feel free to lower your voice a bit.) Whether you normally have these times or not, get ready because today is one of those days! Think for a moment . . .

* God chose to set His love on you.
* God gave you the gift of faith to believe in Him and to be His child.
* Your heavenly Father blessed you with every good thing you have, every good thing you are, and every good thing you have experienced.
* He blessed you with salvation, certain skills, the ability to reason, and countless physical blessings.
* God has been faithful to you in the past—and by nature He cannot break a promise—and He promises to be faithful in the future.

God's love is manifest in our lives in infinite ways!

So take a break from your problems today and praise Him for His compassion, patience, faithfulness, mercy, and grace! He has mercifully not given you what you deserve: death for your sin. He has graciously given you what you *don't* deserve: salvation and eternal life! So today, let's sing praise to God! (Ah, go ahead . . . sing louder. He's worth it!)

LORD, WE ARE AMAZED BY HOW GOOD YOU ARE TO US. WE CANNOT HELP BUT BE FILLED WITH JOY AS WE THINK OF HOW MUCH YOU HAVE BLESSED US. THANK YOU FOR GIVING US A HEART OF GRATITUDE AND FOR ALLOWING US THIS TIME TO SING PRAISES TO YOU!

The servants of the Lord are to sing His praises in this life to the world's end; and in the next life, world without end.
JOHN BOYS

LOVE IN ACTION

1. Talk together about all the things you love about the Lord. Take five turns each praising God for something He has done for you.

2. Pick a few worship songs that you both know by heart. Take a few minutes and sing them out loud together. (If you don't know any, then just whistle to His glory!)

IN PURSUIT OF EXCELLENCE

An excellent wife is the crown of her husband,
But she who causes shame is like rottenness in his bones.

PROVERBS 12:4

ID YOU EVER WEAR a birthday crown in elementary school? Probably so—unless you were cursed with a summertime birthday!

Well, husbands, you have an opportunity to wear an even grander crown, that of a wife who serves the Lord in all she does. The Lord God deserves excellence in all we do, and when a wife pursues that goal in order to bring glory to the Lord, she will be "the crown of her husband." What an honor for her—and for him!

So what is an excellent wife? Here are a few basics:

* She supports her husband by being his helpmate (Genesis 2:20). Not afraid of hard work, she handles her responsibilities so capably that her husband needn't worry.
* By encouraging him and showing him God's grace, she helps her husband become the man of God that the Lord desires him to be.
* She is a loyal friend to him and a faithful prayer warrior. She speaks wisely and acts kindly in the home and outside.

Finally, remember that when God calls, He empowers! His standards of excellence are high for husbands as well as wives, and His limitless power—given to us through His indwelling Spirit—will help us in our pursuit of excellence.

> Lord, help us love one another so that each of us can become the person of God You want us to be and, consequently, the life-long partner You desire to bless us with.

LOVE IN ACTION

1. Okay, husbands, speak the truth in love as you encourage your wife by thanking her for all the ways she supports you in your day-to-day life as well as in your pursuit of Christlikeness.

2. Wives, ask your husband to share an area, if any, where you may be hindering him instead of helping in his pursuit of Christ. Husbands, be sure to be extra gentle as you encourage your wife to excel still more. Bring the conversation to the Lord in humble prayer.

God save us all from wives who are angels in the streets, saints in the church, and devils at home.
CHARLES
SPURGEON

Draw Near! | *We do not have a High Priest who cannot sympathize with our weaknesses, but was in all points tempted as we are, yet without sin.*
HEBREWS 4:15

IT'S A TRUTH YOU may have heard many times before, but camp on it right now. Really think about it . . .

The God of all creation—who formed and sustains the entire universe—became a human being. He took on a body just like yours.

He was born.

He grew.

He got hungry.

He got thirsty.

He got tired.

He cried.

He prayed.

And His moral character was tempted much worse than we can ever imagine.

Jesus was fully human as well as fully divine.

And these are some of the reasons that He completely understands whatever you are experiencing on this earth. He understands what it is to be lonely and misunderstood. He knows what it is to be rejected, betrayed, and abandoned.

Jesus knows your weaknesses, and that is why you can go to Him confident that He will extend grace and mercy to you. His grace will cover your future failures just as His grace has covered your past failures. His mercy is with you now, and it will be for all your tomorrows.

LORD JESUS, YOU UNDERSTAND MY WEAKNESSES, AND
YOU KNOW WHAT IT IS LIKE TO FACE TEMPTATION. I
PRAISE YOU BECAUSE YOU CAN HELP ME STAND STRONG
WHEN I'M TEMPTED, THAT YOU WILL BE MERCIFUL WHEN
I FALL, AND THAT YOUR GRACE WILL ALWAYS COVER ME.
THANK YOU, JESUS! THANK YOU.

*You may
look for
encouragement
from Christ
in everything
but sin.*
SAMUEL
ANNESLEY

LOVE IN ACTION

1. Spend some time together in prayer right now and draw near to Your heavenly Father. Marvel over and thank Him for the fact that Jesus became human and totally understands whatever you're going through.

2. What temptations are you facing? For what do you need to ask God's mercy? His grace? Do so now.

WHAT ARE YOU WEARING?
| PART 1 |

Put off all these: anger, wrath, malice, blasphemy, filthy language out of your mouth. Do not lie to one another, since you have put off the old man with his deeds, and have put on the new man who is renewed in knowledge according to the image of Him who created him.

COLOSSIANS 3:8–10

AAHHHH . . . . It's a day at home, and that means your favorite pair of jeans and that soft, old sweatshirt . . . We wear the comfortable stuff around the house, don't we?

That's fine—unless we're talking about the comfortable stuff from our old sin nature. You know, the short temper, the mean and unnecessary comment, the half-truth you told over the weekend. These actions aren't appropriate anywhere, including around the house.

We aren't to act the way we used to act before we named Jesus our Lord and Savior. As Colossians 3:8 says, we need to keep putting off our old self because God calls us to holiness. Look at the specifics we are to put off:

* *Anger*—volcanic eruptions of rage
* *Wrath*—the desire to punish or exact revenge
* *Malice*—the desire to cause someone pain, injury, or distress
* *Blasphemy*—slander spewed about others
* *Filthy language*—coarse speech that is impure and offensive
* *Lies*—untruths and half-truths that benefit us

Perhaps some or all of these behaviors characterized our life at one point, but the Holy Spirit has been at work in us since we became a child of God. And He continues to work in us to renew us, to make us more like Jesus each day, so let's "train yourself to be godly" (1 Timothy 4:7 NIV), and glorify the Lord by putting off those old, dirty clothes.

> LORD GOD, THAT "OLD MAN" IS TOO OFTEN ALIVE AND WELL IN ME—AND WHILE I MAY DO A DECENT JOB WHEN I'M OUT IN PUBLIC, AT HOME HE TOO OFTEN HAS HIS WAY WITH ME. FORGIVE ME, LORD, AND HELP ME TO DELIBERATELY AND CONSISTENTLY PUT HIM OFF, ESPECIALLY WHEN I'M AT HOME.

LOVE IN ACTION

1. Grab that favorite pair of grubby jeans and that much-loved old sweatshirt and go on a hike with your beloved. No agenda for this outing! The assignment? Simply enjoy!

2. Which component of the old man do you most need to work on? Confess it here—and ask the Lord for help. Also consider what triggers this behavior so that you can cut it off sooner rather than later.

We must not account sin a pleasure; but a thing to be hated by a Christian as deadly poison, or to be avoided as a putrid carcass.
JOHN DAVENPORT

WHAT ARE YOU WEARING?
| PART 2 |

*As the elect of God, holy and beloved, put on tender mercies,
kindness, humility, meekness, longsuffering; bearing with one another,
and forgiving one another, if anyone has a complaint against another;
even as Christ forgave you, so you also must do.*

COLOSSIANS 3:12–13

I DON'T HAVE A thing to wear!"

It's quite likely that wives have said those words and husbands have heard them more times than either cares to remember.

Well, as you clean out your closet per Colossians 3:8–10 (throwing out the old stuff from your sin nature), and you feel you simply don't have a thing to wear, then we have good news! Here's your new wardrobe:

* *Tender mercies*—showing kindness and compassion when they're least deserved
* *Kindness*—extending sympathetic and gentle thoughts and deeds
* *Humility*—viewing others as better than ourselves; we more easily defer to treating them with honor and respect
* *Meekness*—showing a mild and submissive spirit and attitude toward others
* *Longsuffering*—exhibiting patience and endurance in drawn-out and trying situations
* *Bearing with one another*—willingly enduring other people's irritating ways and shortcomings
* *Forgiving one another*—releasing another's offense without ill feelings or keeping score

These traits are the fruits—the byproducts—of the Holy Spirit living within us and making us more like Jesus. And as we, who are God's elect people, continue to grow in these godly traits, we will more clearly reflect the character of our Lord and Savior—an upgrade in our wardrobe that our spouse will undoubtedly appreciate!

> LORD GOD, ONLY BY YOUR GRACE AND ONLY THROUGH YOUR SPIRIT CAN I LIVE OUT THESE TRAITS. AS I YIELD TO YOUR TRANSFORMING WORK, HELP ME BE A MORE CHRISTLIKE SPOUSE.

If conversion to Christianity makes no improvement in a man's outward actions . . . then I think we must suspect that his "conversion" was largely imaginary.
C. S. LEWIS

LOVE IN ACTION

1. Think through the seven godly "fruits" previously listed. Which one or two best describe your spouse? Encourage each other by sharing the Christlike qualities you most see in your life-mate.

2. Which piece of this godly "wardrobe" are you wearing least often? Confess it here—and ask the Lord either to help the scratchy newness wear off or to help you put it on more often. What will you do this week to be sure to put on this piece of clothing? It really will go with everything!

THE COMMISSION'S STILL GREAT

He said to them, "Go into all the world
and preach the gospel to every creature."

MARK 16:15

WHEN HAVE YOU HAD a hard time keeping a secret? Was it when the news was especially good? When you knew you'd be adding joy to the hearer's life?

Why, then, do we Christians often have such an easy time keeping the gospel a secret? We find ourselves less than comfortable trying to talk about the gospel to people who don't know the truth about Jesus, people who would find forgiveness of their sins, purpose for their days on earth, and the promise of life eternal very good news.

God has commissioned, or commanded, us to do just that. Even in our media-saturated culture, He still uses personal relationships—believer to unbeliever—to communicate the life- and eternity-changing truth about the person and work of Jesus.

Interestingly, often what we say most clearly about Jesus comes not from our words, but from how we live our lives. In other words, if we tell someone that Jesus has transformed us, and we don't look too transformed, why should that person listen?

So what do your unbelieving family members and friends see in you and your marriage? In this fallen world of lying, cheating, adultery, and divorce, a Christ-centered marriage can provide us with incredible opportunities to talk about Jesus. Our marriage even offers pictures of the gospel:

* Our committed love for our spouse reflects God's everlasting love for us (Jeremiah 31:3).
* We forgive each other just as God forgives our sins (1 John 1:9).

* We are faithful to our spouse; Christ is faithful to us (1 Corinthians 1:9).

So when people who've been watching your marriage ask you the secret of your success, be ready to share the truth. You might start with, "It's no secret. It's God's grace!"

> LORD GOD, IT'S AMAZING HOW A MARRIAGE ROOTED IN YOU CAN OFFER THE WORLD A PICTURE OF THE CHURCH'S RELATIONSHIP WITH JESUS. PLEASE WORK IN OUR HEARTS, LORD, SO THAT OUR MARRIAGE REFLECTS YOU TO THE NONBELIEVERS AROUND US.

The glory of the gospel is that when the church is absolutely different from the world, she invariably attracts it.
MARTYN LLOYD-JONES

LOVE IN ACTION

1. Invite over for dinner a non-Christian couple you've wanted to get to know better. Just be yourselves and let your actions preach the gospel to them. All the while, pray that the Lord would provide opportunities to speak of the person and work of Jesus Christ.

2. Review the basics of the gospel, and practice how you would explain the good news to a nonbeliever. You might even practice saying the words out loud.

MAYBE NOT SO BAD AFTER ALL

You meant evil against me; but God meant it for good.

GENESIS 50:20

EVER HAD SOMEONE DO something really nasty to you?

Maybe they cheated off of you in school, and then laughed when you were the one who got suspended. Or maybe they spread a lie about you, and it cost you your job.

Think back on all the bad things that have happened to you, specifically the ones that were caused by other people. As painful and frustrating as those situations may have been, if you are a Christian, God, in His infinite wisdom and power, allowed each of those events—even the sin of others—to happen for your own good (Romans 8:28).

Take Joseph . . . He had a bad experience—and in his case it was caused by his brothers. Joseph's brothers burned with jealousy toward him and planned to kill him. At the last minute, however, they chose to sell him to a caravan of travelers who eventually sold Joseph into Egyptian slavery. There, he was falsely accused of sin and thrown into prison.

Wow, that sounds like some bad days! But if you know the rest of the story, you know that from prison, Joseph was summoned by Pharaoh and was eventually put in charge of the entire kingdom (Genesis 37– 41).

As painful as the experience was for Joseph, God was clearly working all things together for Joseph's ultimate good—and for Isreal's ultimate good!

Now look back at your life together, past and present. Maybe you have been or are currently going through circumstances that seem wrong or unfair. As you think through these situations, always remember that God is working His perfect and providential plan in your life. Choose to rest in God's plan and commit as a couple to trust in His Sovereignty.

As we reflect on the past, Lord, we know that You are a sovereign God and You always have our best in mind. Please give us the faith to trust in You always and to not react in vengeance when others do evil against us. Instead, help us to show them Your love.

LOVE IN ACTION

1. For what specific situation in your life right now is today's devotional especially encouraging? Thank God for being a source of hope and for reminding you of that truth today.

God would never permit evil, if He could not bring good out of evil.
St. Augustine

2. Remember together a time when God's sovereign hand was obvious in your marriage relationship or in certain circumstances in your life together. Let that example of God's faithfulness encourage you to trust Him all the more.

BEST DRESSED
| ARMOR OF GOD **PART 1** |

Be strong in the Lord and in the power of His might.
Put on the whole armor of God, that you may be able
to stand against the wiles of the devil.

EPHESIANS 6:10–11

HAVE YOU EVER LOOKED down the street and wondered why some people's marriages seem so easy?

A couple of things come to mind. First, you don't know their story. Many of us can be Academy Award-winning performers in public.

Second, if they don't know the Lord, the enemy may be leaving them alone. Unfortunately, the converse of that is also true: if a husband and wife know the Lord and are committed to having a marriage that glorifies Him, the enemy will go after them—big-time. This deceiver will make us wonder if it's worth living life God's way and, more specifically, worth living out our marriage God's way. In fact, the more we grow in our faith, the more frequently and intensely we may be attacked.

So what are we to do? How are we to stand strong in the Lord?

Believe it or not, the answer is in our clothing. Yes, our clothing. We need to be the better dressed—better dressed *spiritually*—and that means putting on "the whole armor of God," which we'll be addressing piece by piece in the following pages.

The devil is alive and well, and he loves to attack God's people. Only if we are "strong in the Lord and in the power of His might" can we prevail. When Satan attacks, we are to respond to his temptations with God's truth, as Jesus modeled in the wilderness (Luke 4:1–13). We are to rely on the

Holy Spirit for discernment and fortitude as we look to God's powerful and loving protection. In His grace, God will give us His strength to "stand against the wiles of the devil."

> LORD, EVEN THOUGH I KNOW I WILL FAIL, IT'S OFTEN A TEMPTATION FOR ME TO FIGHT SPIRITUAL BATTLES IN MY OWN STRENGTH. BUT WHEN IT'S MY MARRIAGE THAT'S AT STAKE, I DON'T WANT TO TAKE ANY RISKS: TEACH ME TO "BE STRONG IN [YOU] AND IN THE POWER OF [YOUR] MIGHT."

Without the Spirit of God we can do nothing. We are as ships without wind or chariots without steeds; like branches without sap, we are withered.
C. H. SPURGEON

LOVE IN ACTION

1. Read through Luke 4:1–13 together. Then spend a few minutes talking about Jesus' model of resisting temptation. What did He do to ward off Satan's attacks?

2. Watch a good war movie together—like *Sands of Iwo Jima* or *The Bridge on the River Kwai*. Afterward, discuss the strategy you two have in place to fight the enemy.

IDENTIFY THE ENEMY
| ARMOR OF GOD **PART 2** |

*We do not wrestle against flesh and blood, but against principalities,
against powers, against the rulers of the darkness of this age,
against spiritual hosts of wickedness in the heavenly places.*

EPHESIANS 6:12

WHICH SEEMS MORE REAL—THE shattered pieces of crystal or the gravity that took over when the vase was bumped?

We human beings usually find the seen and tangible much more real than the unseen and intangible. And in our marriage that tendency can lead us to consider our (seen and tangible) spouse as the enemy when, in actuality, our enemy is Satan and his demons, the unseen and intangible.

In many cases, our own fallen flesh is enough to cause marital strife, but we need to remember that we're also in a spiritual battle against supernatural evil. It's all too easy to blame our troubles on our spouse because he or she is right there, in plain sight, but as we seek to stand strong against spiritual warfare, we must continually remember that we are on the same team, fighting the same common enemy.

Having identified the enemy, let's consider the best strategy. Simply put, we are to pursue a holy life that fails to provide Satan with any opportunities to settle in. As James put it centuries ago, "Submit to God. Resist the devil and he will flee from you" (James 4:7).

So remember that your spouse is on your side. We need to support each other, but if we act like enemies, it will be a victory for Satan. As the Scriptures say, "Though one may be overpowered, two can defend themselves" (Ecclesiastes 4:12 NIV).

Pray without ceasing for your marriage and for each other. Sink your roots deep into the Word of God. God gives us all we need to stand strong. It's our job to use—and use well—the tools He provides.

LORD GOD, THANK YOU THAT WE DON'T FIGHT OUR BATTLES ALONE. THANK YOU THAT YOUR HOLY SPIRIT LIVES WITHIN US AND THAT YOU'VE PROVIDED IN EACH OF US A FELLOW SOLDIER IN THE BATTLE. KEEP US STRONGLY UNITED AS WE FIGHT THE ENEMY AND, WE PRAY, BRING YOU THE ULTIMATE GLORY!

LOVE IN ACTION

1. Discuss together what you can do when the battle is raging to remind each other that you're on the same team.

2. What does it mean to you that your spouse is "a fellow soldier in the battle"? Spend some time in prayer thanking God for this partner and pray for each other's strength and endurance.

If God were not my friend, Satan would not be so much my enemy.
THOMAS BROOKS

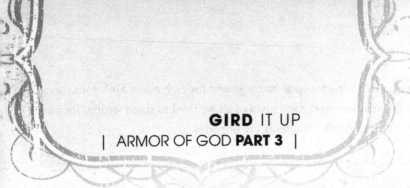

GIRD IT UP
| ARMOR OF GOD **PART 3** |

. . . having girded your waist with truth . . .

EPHESIANS 6:14

MOST OF US, to some degree, like to be fashionable. And even for those of us who don't give a second thought to what we wear, it is likely that our spouse would prefer that we did!

In the battle against Satan, however, there's no time for a spiritual fashion statement because each of us needs to don the same pieces of armor. Only then will we fight in God's strength and for His glory.

You may be surprised to learn that, in Paul's day, a key piece of a soldier's armor was his belt. In order to run swiftly, the soldier needed his belt to gather his loose undergarments. Also, if the belt were not cinched tightly, none of his other pieces of armor would be secure.

For God's soldier, the *belt of truth*, the Word of God, is equally important to living a life that honors Him. Romans 12:2 tells us that in order to win the battle, we must be transformed by the renewing of our mind. And God's Word is the instrument the Holy Spirit uses to work that change in us.

As believers study the Bible, a powerful dynamic is at work: the Holy Spirit illumines the Scriptures and teaches us God's truth. This life-changing truth begins to become apparent in our lives as the Holy Spirit molds our character to be more like Christ. Just as a car needs gas to power it, we need God's Word, and the Holy Spirit's power, to live victoriously.

Truth is also key to whether your battle for your marriage will be won or lost, but be encouraged that you have the best weapon for defeating the enemy—God's Word. Commit yourselves to personal Bible study and praying together. Then enjoy the many blessings that come from having a marriage built on the foundation of the Word of God.

> LORD, PLEASE GIVE US NOT ONLY THE DESIRE BUT
> THE DISCIPLINE TO READ GOD'S WORD EACH DAY
> AND TO YIELD TO YOUR SPIRIT AS HE APPLIES
> YOUR TRUTH TO OUR LIVES.

The chief weapon we ought to use in resisting Satan is the Bible.
J. C. RYLE

LOVE IN ACTION

1. King David said, "Your word I have hidden in my heart, that I might not sin against You" (Psalm 119:11). Choose a passage to hide in your heart (memorize) and recite to each other tomorrow.

2. Tell of a situation or time when remembering a passage of Scripture kept you a truthful person.

LIVING IT OUT

| ARMOR OF GOD **PART 4** |

. . . having put on the breastplate of righteousness . . .

EPHESIANS 6:14

WITH OUR BELT of truth secured tightly, now we need the *breast-plate of righteousness.*

The breastplate was a large piece of leather, or sometimes metal, that was fixed to the chest to protect the heart, lungs, and other vital organs during a hand-to-hand sword fight.

By God's grace, every Christian has such breastplate protection from eternal condemnation because of the righteousness of Jesus Christ. Jesus fulfilled God's law perfectly, and the moment you put your faith in Him, this accomplishment was credited to your account, as if you yourself had lived His perfect life.

Putting on the breastplate of righteousness means pursuing holiness in every aspect of our life so that we may bring glory to the Savior because of what He has done on our behalf. And as we pursue righteousness, we will be able, in God's strength, to defend ourselves against the assaults of temptation from the enemy.

Even in the best of circumstances, life can be difficult. But as we grow in our righteousness, we will not only honor our Lord, but we will be blessed with greater joy in our marriage.

So encourage each other toward genuine, Christlike, holy living and may you and your spouse be found worthy servants of the Lord, walking faithfully in His ways (Ephesians 4:1). Jesus, who paid the ultimate price for you, is worth it—and so is your marriage.

> WHAT A GREAT PRIVILEGE YOU GIVE US, LORD, TO BE
> ABLE TO ENCOURAGE EACH OTHER TO LIVE RIGHTEOUSLY
> FOR YOUR GLORY. LORD, LET US BE DILIGENT IN OUR
> DAILY WALK WITH YOU AND IN OUR COMMITMENT TO
> EACH OTHER. AND MAY WE REMAIN HUMBLE IN OUR
> UNDERSTANDING OF WHO YOU ARE AND WHAT YOU
> HAVE DONE FOR US.

LOVE IN ACTION

1. Share with each other those areas of your life that need to be better protected by the breastplate of righteousness.

2. Commit to praying for each other at three set times over the next two days and ask the Lord to help your spouse walk in holiness. Consider making this a regular practice.

When holiness is pressed upon us we are prone to think that it is a doctrine calculated for angels and spirits whose dwelling is not with flesh. But when we read the lives of them that excelled in holiness, though they were persons of like passions with ourselves, the conviction is wonderful and powerful.
COTTON MATHER

CHECK OUT MY NEW SHOES!
| ARMOR OF GOD **PART 5** |

. . . having shod your feet with the preparation of the gospel of peace . . .

EPHESIANS 6:15

DON'T YOU JUST LOVE getting a new pair of shoes? Maybe the perfect pumps to go with that perfect dress. Or maybe a sweet pair of air-cushioned running shoes—even if all you do is run to the couch to watch the playoffs.

Our footwear can be a fashion statement, but the right shoes can also help us accomplish our goals. You wouldn't wear pumps to run a marathon, and you wouldn't wear running shoes with the new dress (although you'd probably like to sometimes).

In wartime two thousand years ago, the right footwear was critical. In those days, Roman soldiers would drive nails through the soles of their boots, and the points of the nails would give them traction, much like our athletic cleats.

In our day, as we battle the enemy, we need to wear the right *spiritual* shoes so that our feet may be firmly planted as we resist Satan's attacks. And our traction comes only from the gospel.

As believers, we stand firm knowing that through Christ, though we were once His enemy, we are now at peace with God and He is on our side. We can confidently trust that He is our Defender, Protector, and Victor, and nothing can separate us from His love (see Romans 8:38–39).

And true peace with others is only possible if we first have this peace or *shalom* with God. The Hebrew word *shalom* means "completeness, wholeness, safety, and fullness." When we each know this *shalom* with God, then, regardless of any battle raging without, we can know God's peace within our marriage.

So may our homes be blessed with peace as we live in completeness, wholeness, and abundance in Christ. And may we be that kind of blessing to our spouse.

> WE WANT OUR HOME TO REFLECT THE PEACE WE EACH HAVE WITH YOU, LORD. THANK YOU THAT WE ARE ABLE TO STAND IN THE CONFIDENCE THAT, AS OUR DEFENDER AND PROTECTOR, YOU WILL HELP OUR MARRIAGE WITHSTAND ANY ATTACK.

God cannot give us happiness and peace apart from Himself, because it is not there. There is no such thing.
C. S. LEWIS

LOVE IN ACTION

1. When have you felt protected or been defended by someone? What does that experience illustrate about the role God wants to play in your life?

2. Find a place of peace for the two of you to retreat to—for an hour, an overnighter, a weekend. During that getaway, take some time to thank God together for the peace that comes from the gospel.

SHIELDED BY FAITH
| ARMOR OF GOD **PART 6** |

*. . . above all, taking the shield of faith with which
you will be able to quench all the fiery darts of the wicked one.*

EPHESIANS 6:16

THERE'S A SCENE IN the beginning of *Raiders of the Lost Ark* when our hero, with golden idol in hand, runs for his life as poisonous darts come at him from all directions. Of course our hero emerges unscathed—or there would not have been a billion dollar movie franchise—but that scene is still symbolic of our own spiritual lives: we carry our own idols and run on our own strength as the enemy shoots his fiery darts directly at us.

Well, life is not a Hollywood fantasy, but we can take great comfort in knowing that, in His grace, God has given us a shield to protect us from Satan's attacks.

Our *shield of faith* is the continual trust we put in God because we understand who He is and what He has done for us.

The deceiver promises us pleasure and fulfillment apart from God, and our sin comes when we fall victim to his deceptions. We may be tempted to think that having an adulterous affair or telling a little white lie to get a promotion at work will bring us more meaning and greater happiness. But since such desires are in direct opposition to the Scriptures, they are clearly from the evil one.

Throughout life and marriage, anger, pride, envy, sexual immorality, and myriad of other temptations often come when we least expect them. But our shield of faith—our actively trusting in God, His Word, and the saving work of Jesus Christ—is our defense in the battle.

Protect yourself and protect your marriage. Grab your shield and don't let go!

> LORD, WE ARE COMMITTED TO HOLDING UP OUR SHIELDS OF FAITH AND PROTECTING OURSELVES AGAINST ENEMY ATTACKS. PLEASE KEEP US FROM THROWING FIERY DARTS AT EACH OTHER AND ENABLE US TO LIVE ACCORDING TO YOUR WORD.

We must not count temptation a strange thing. "The disciple is not greater than his master, nor the servant than his lord." If Satan came to Christ, he will also come to Christians.
J. C. RYLE

LOVE IN ACTION

1. Go bowling or play darts, croquet, or laser tag. Whatever you choose, realize and remember that Satan has an even better aim than you do. You need your shield of faith!

2. Alone with God, ask Him to show you with what darts, if any, you've wounded your spouse. Then ask his or her forgiveness—and God's.

PROTECT YOUR NOGGIN!
| ARMOR OF GOD **PART 7** |

And take the helmet of salvation . . .

EPHESIANS 6:17

HELMETS.

Football players wear them.

Combat soldiers do as well.

Laws even require motorcyclists to have one on.

We all understand the importance of protecting our noggins, so it doesn't take a genius to understand the importance of helmets.

As Christians, we too must guard our heads, which is why the Lord tells us that wherever we go and whatever we do, we are to take *the helmet of salvation.*

This helmet is the rock-solid reality that once we are Christ's, we are His forever. From the moment Jesus saves us, we have complete security in knowing that He has saved us for all eternity. Nothing and no one can ever take away our salvation. Not even Satan.

The enemy attacks us with discouragement and doubt. When we struggle with sin, when we or people we know face trials, or when we don't see the changes in our marriage we would like to see, we can feel despair.

It is during these times of discouragement that we most need our helmet of salvation. If we don't trust in our eternal security we can easily believe Satan rather than God, and we may find ourselves lacking diligence in the battle and even questioning whether our efforts are in vain. These doubts also affect our relationship with others as we will tend to focus on circumstances rather than keeping our eyes on Christ and His promises. If that weren't enough, our marriage can also be undermined as the enemy will try to prompt us to doubt our spouse's forgiveness or love.

So make sure you aren't giving Satan a foothold by doubting God's love—and make sure to wear your helmet. Every day.

> LORD, WE CONFESS THERE ARE TIMES WE DOUBT YOU AND YOUR GOODNESS TO US. WE GET DISCOURAGED WHEN WE FOCUS ON OURSELVES OR OUR CIRCUMSTANCES. PLEASE HELP US REMEMBER THAT YOU HAVE SAVED US AND WILL KEEP US SAVED. GIVE US CONFIDENCE IN YOU AS WE STRIVE TO LIVE FAITHFULLY FOR EACH OTHER.

LOVE IN ACTION

1. Brainstorm together what the two of you can do to protect yourself from discouragement and doubt. Maybe it's time to hide another verse of Scripture in your hearts.

2. Who in your church family could use some encouragement? Start by praying for that person and then make a call or send a card of encouragement. And don't forget to point him or her to God's unfailing promises.

Assurance will assist us in all duties; it will arm us against all temptations; it will answer all objections; it will sustain us in all conditions.
EDWARD REYNOLDS

EVER READ A SWORD?
| ARMOR OF GOD **PART 8** |

And take . . . the sword of the Spirit, which is the word of God . . .

EPHESIANS 6:17

A S WE'VE SEEN, IN preparation for battle, an ancient soldier would put on his breastplate and secure his loose clothing with his belt. He would strap on his ground-gripping boots, don his helmet, and pick up his shield.

But no warrior's armor was complete without his sword. And for the Christian, the sword of the Spirit is none other than the Holy Scriptures.

How can we stand strong against the enemy? How can we live a pure and holy life? By living our life according to the Word of God (see Psalm 119:11).

In 2 Timothy 2:15, the apostle Paul put it this way: "Be diligent to present yourself approved to God, a worker who does not need to be ashamed, rightly dividing the word of truth." Simply put, we need to work hard so that we can accurately understand the Bible.

It has often been said that bank tellers learn to identify counterfeit money by handling and studying the real thing. That same principle works for us: the more we handle God's truth, the more easily we'll recognize the lies of the adversary. The better we know God's Word, the more easily we will be able to swing our sword of the Spirit and defeat the enemy.

So take the challenge. God will transform your marriage as both of you make knowing His Word your number one priority. His Spirit will use that knowledge to change each of you into the person He created you to be, as well as experience the unity and intimacy He intends for you to experience.

Just be ready for the incredible blessings you will experience as a couple as you read His Word and obey!

THANK YOU, LORD, FOR GIVING US THE SWORD OF THE SPIRIT—

> THE SCRIPTURES. HELP US BECOME STUDENTS OF YOUR WORD AS WE HAVE NEVER BEEN BEFORE. AND THANK YOU FOR YOUR HOLY SPIRIT, WHO HELPS US UNDERSTAND YOUR TRUTH AS WE READ IT.

In opposition…to all the suggestions of the devil, the sole, simple, and sufficient answer is the word of God. This puts to flight all the powers of darkness.

CHARLES HODGE

LOVE IN ACTION

1. Is this a season of your life when you two can teach Sunday school together and help the next generation learn to wield the sword of the Spirit? Pray about it and see what God says.

2. What Bible study plan, if any, are you currently doing together? Individual study is crucial, but shared study will make you and your marriage even stronger.

ARE YOU FORGETTING **SOMETHING?**
| ARMOR OF GOD **PART 9** |

. . . praying always with all prayer and supplication
in the Spirit, being watchful to this end with all perseverance
and supplication for all the saints.

EPHESIANS 6:18

WE HAVE BEEN CONVINCED that we are in a battle.

We have understood who the battle is against.

We have seen the armor we must wear.

But before we march headstrong toward the enemy, there is one absolutely critical piece of equipment, without which, we will face certain defeat.

Prayer.

For the believer, prayer is as essential to our spiritual well-being as food and water are to our physical. If we try to live our Christian lives without prayer, we will simply lose the battle.

The Lord, in His grace, commands us to pray, but praying is also a privilege. And as our verse today says, we have the blessing of being able to commune with our Lord not only for *our* needs, but for the needs of our fellow soldiers in Christ.

If you find your prayer life is lacking (and how few of us would claim otherwise), let's commit to spending at least a small amount of time each day in prayer with our spouse. By God's grace and with our discipline, our prayer lives can gradually grow and grow until we are outright prayer warriors. The bottom line is, wherever we are in our prayer lives, let's excel still more!

We have taken up our armor, and we are standing strong in the battle. Now let's pray as though our spiritual lives depend on it . . . because they do.

LORD, IT'S OFTEN EASIER TO READ ABOUT PRAYER OR TO FEEL GUILTY ABOUT NOT PRAYING THAN IT IS TO ACTUALLY PRAY. FORGIVE ME FOR NOT JUST DOING IT, FOR NOT PRAYING FOR MY SPOUSE, OUR MARRIAGE, AND OUR GROWTH TOWARD CHRISTLIKENESS. MAY I PERSEVERE AND PRAY WITH HOPE FOR THE GOOD PLANS YOU HAVE FOR OUR MARRIAGE.

LOVE IN ACTION

1. Okay, it's not your thing . . . but why not grab a spiral binder or a legal pad, and—voilà!—you have a prayer journal or log or whatever unintimidating name you want to give it. Then, together, keep track of your prayers and God's answers. This black-and-white evidence of God's work can be a real faith builder.

2. What keeps you from praying? Busyness? Sleepiness? Lack of confidence? Something else? What will you do to overcome one of these roadblocks this week?

To be a Christian without prayer is no more possible than to be alive without breathing.
MARTIN LUTHER

WEE LITTLE MAN WAS HE

He sought to see who Jesus was, but could not because of the crowd,
for he was of short stature. So he ran ahead and climbed up into a
sycamore tree to see Him, for He was going to pass that way.

LUKE 19:3

G ET DOWN FROM THAT tree before you hurt yourself!"
When we were kids, most of us probably heard that once or twice.

Kids do a lot of crazy things in the name of fun, and parents, all too often, have to be the "bad cop." Kids are scolded for chasing a ball onto the street, reprimanded for running with scissors, and given a firm lecture for not using better judgment when choosing to climb a tree. Obviously, in spite of what kids may think, parents do this out of love for their precious little ones.

For one particular "little one," the scene was entirely different. When the tax collector, Zacchaeus, climbed a tree to see Jesus, no one seemed to care if the "vertically challenged" man fell and broke his neck. For that matter, Zacchaeus probably didn't think much about it himself. At that moment, his safety—and perhaps his dignity—took a back seat, as nothing was going to prevent him from seeing the Savior who was passing by.

We don't know exactly what Zacchaeus was thinking when Jesus singled him out and announced that He must stay in Zacchaeus' house. But we do know the results: Zacchaeus immediately placed his trust in the Lord and was a changed man (Luke 19:1–10). What joy when Jesus Christ has a divine appointment with a sinner!

An ordinary sycamore tree was the sight where Jesus extended His grace to Zacchaeus. And wherever you are today, Jesus is making that same offer to you.

If you've had that divine appointment with Christ, rejoice in His grace. If you haven't, then be like Zacchaeus: humble yourself and do whatever you must do in order to see the Lord.

> LORD, THANK YOU THAT YOU EXTEND YOUR LOVE TO US EVEN THOUGH WE ARE SO UNWORTHY. EVEN AFTER OUR DIVINE APPOINTMENT WITH YOU, THANK YOU THAT YOU STILL BLESS US WITH YOUR GRACE. MAY WE ALWAYS REJOICE IN YOUR GOODNESS!

Christ is . . . not primarily an example for faith but the object of faith.
J. GRESHAM MACHEN

LOVE IN ACTION

1. Put on your walking shoes! Yep, go outside together. Enjoy the fresh air, the company, and the variety of trees God made.

2. Think back on your divine appointment with Jesus, whether it was forty years or forty seconds ago. Recall as many details as possible—and praise God!

THE VERTICAL
AND THE **HORIZONTAL**

If there is any consolation in Christ, if any comfort of love,
if any fellowship of the Spirit, if any affection and mercy,
fulfill my joy by being like-minded, having the same love,
being of one accord, of one mind.

PHILIPPIANS 2:1–2

HAVE YOU EVER CONSIDERED how the vertical can impact the horizontal? Specifically, do you appreciate that the stronger your relationship is with Jesus (the vertical), the smoother your relationships will be with other Christians (the horizontal)? Here are four truths:

* *Consolation in Christ*: As believers, we take great encouragement in Jesus' rule over our lives.
* *Comfort of Love*: The Lord's gentle closeness compels us to tenderly love those around us.
* *Fellowship of the Spirit*: We are partners with our fellow believers, who, like us, have the Holy Spirit living inside of them and will be spending eternity with us in heaven.
* *Affection and Mercy*: Our heavenly God has such fatherly love and affection for us. He continually extends infinite mercy to His children.

If you and your spouse each have a relationship with Jesus, then you are called to be like-minded in extending the same gentle love to one another that our merciful Christ has extended to each of you.

What a great thought to hold onto—that as we strive for closer intimacy with the Lord (vertical), the more united we will be with our spouse (horizontal).

> LORD GOD, THANK YOU THAT ANY INVESTMENT IN MY RELATIONSHIP WITH YOU IS ALSO AN INVESTMENT IN MY MARRIAGE AND THAT GROWING IN LOVE FOR YOU WILL HELP ME BETTER LOVE MY SPOUSE. I PRAY THE INTIMATE LOVE I EXPERIENCE WITH YOU WILL EXTEND TO MY RELATIONSHIP WITH FELLOW BELIEVERS, ESPECIALLY MY SPOUSE.

What! At peace with the Father, and at war with His children? It cannot be.
JOHN FLAVEL

LOVE IN ACTION

1. Talk together about what factors can keep the two of you from "being like-minded" in Christ. Then come up with ideas for how to conquer or avoid those negative factors. What difference, for instance, would humility make in like-mindedness?

2. Reread today's verse and take a few minutes to pray together. Specifically thank the Lord for extending to us the four foundational truths (consolation in Christ, comfort of love, fellowship of the Spirit, and affection and mercy) found in this passage.

IT'S BEEN HIJACKED!

*Do you not know that your body is the temple of the Holy Spirit
who is in you, whom you have from God, and you are not your own?
For you were bought at a price; therefore glorify God
in your body and in your spirit, which are God's.*

I CORINTHIANS 6:19–20

PERHAPS IN NO OTHER realm are the world's view and God's view in such opposition. The world sees it as "all about me"; God doesn't. The world can view it as dirty; God never does. The world will flaunt it, capitalize on it, and use it as a marketing tool; God wants it honored and protected. In the world's hand, this gift is used destructively and sinfully; God's heart is broken. As you may have guessed, "it" is sex.

God created sex, Satan hijacked it, and, sadly, to some degree we believers have bought into the world's wrong view of sex more than we have the Bible's view.

The Bible's perspective is simple and straightforward: God gave sex to a man and a woman who have entered into a lifelong covenant marriage relationship with each other. That gift is to be celebrated, enjoyed, and—this may surprise some—regarded as an act of worship.

The next time you prepare for that special closeness with your spouse, remember that you are going to worship the Lord. May that perspective prompt you to seek to serve your spouse in the marriage bed. Find out what he or she likes and try to make your time together a beautiful act of worship as you serve him or her. Your doing so is also a step toward God's people taking back this divine gift from the world that has corrupted it. What a delightful way to be His light!

> ALL GOOD GIFTS COME FROM YOU, LORD GOD! WE THANK YOU FOR THE GIFT OF SEX AND ASK YOU TO HELP US BE GOOD STEWARDS OF IT. MAY WE HONOR YOU AND EACH OTHER WHENEVER WE MEET ON THE MARRIAGE BED.

LOVE IN ACTION

1. If you are struggling to know how to please your spouse, don't go to the world for ideas. Talk to each other. If needed, husbands, seek out a godly man and, wives, a godly woman for counsel and prayer.

2. Make some time to talk openly about your sexual relationship and its significance as an act of worship. Listen carefully to what each other has to say, and then spend some time praying about this aspect of your relationship.

Let the wife make her husband glad to come home and let him make her sorry to see him leave.
MARTIN LUTHER

A PICTURE IS WORTH . . .

Scarcely had I passed by them,
When I found the one I love.
I held him and would not let him go,
Until I had brought him to the house of my mother,
And into the chamber of her who conceived me.

SONG OF SOLOMON 3:4

THE SONG OF SOLOMON is filled with vivid pictures of godly, passionate lovemaking between a man and a woman. Its pages offer insight into the celebration of this God-ordained gift to married couples.

The verse above is part of the young bride's dream. This Shulammite woman is anticipating the day when she will become one with her Solomon. In her dream she expresses her total devotion and love for Solomon, repeating four times in the first four verses of chapter 3 the phrase "him whom my soul loves" (NASB).

Solomon will be his bride's exclusive lover, and she understands that their purity is of the utmost importance. She protects herself from her passionate desire for her husband-to-be by setting up barriers to keep herself pure until the day when their physical love would be a righteous and godly act.

We can learn much from this biblical example of a passionate young bride, including the truth that any sexual satisfaction is to come exclusively through our spouse. Any sexual satisfaction experienced either solo or with someone other than our spouse is, simply put, sinful.

So just as the Shulammite woman guarded her purity prior to her marriage, we need to be continually guarding ours now that we are married. In all ways, we must be a one-woman man and a one-man woman. Let the cry of our heart to our spouse be: "I only have eyes for you."

> FATHER, THANK YOU FOR THE FREEING MESSAGE
> THAT PHYSICAL INTIMACY WITHIN THE CONFINES
> OF MARRIAGE IS A BEAUTIFUL GIFT. AND THANK
> YOU, GOD, FOR THE SONG OF SOLOMON'S VIVID
> PICTURE OF WHAT YOU INTEND BIBLICAL SEX TO BE.

First he must choose his love, and then he must love his choice.
HENRY SMITH

LOVE IN ACTION

1. If at all possible, be honest with each other about your reaction to this discussion of sex and the Song of Solomon. What new truth did you learn or what godly perspective were you reminded of?

2. If you struggle to wholeheartedly embrace this picture of godly, biblical sex, take some time to pray. If need be, seek the counsel of a trusted pastor or godly friend. Your spouse will thank you.

ONLY BY GOD'S GRACE

Let your fountain be blessed,
And rejoice with the wife of your youth.
As a loving deer and a graceful doe,
Let her breasts satisfy you at all times;
And always be enraptured with her love.

PROVERBS 5:18–19

THE SONG OF SOLOMON isn't the only place in Scripture where husbands and wives are encouraged to enjoy the blessing of the marriage bed. Here in Proverbs, God calls the husband to make his wife the complete and only focus of his sexual attention. Not an easy assignment in the twenty-first century.

* Paying for milk at the grocery store brings to a man's eyes the almost-clothed cover girl on *Cosmopolitan*.
* Watching his favorite team means seeing many a female body try to sell a variety of products during the commercial breaks.
* Unbelievable images, including powerfully addicting ones, can stream right into the office or home computer.
* Even going to church can invite eyes to stray as devoted Christian women wear low-cut tops, short skirts, and stiletto heels.

What's a red-blooded man to do? And how's a wife to compete?

By God's grace and in His power, husbands and wives are to stay committed to His guidelines for marriage, and here His guidelines come in the form of a command: Husband, make your wife the sole focus of your sexual attention. Choose to find your emotional and physical enjoyment in her—and in her alone. Consider that the word *enraptured* means to be drunk on love for your wife—and having all sexual passions under the control of your love for her. And only her body is to satisfy any sexual urge you have. Not a bad command to have to work on obeying, is it?

LORD GOD, PLEASE BLESS AND PROTECT MY MARRIAGE BED. PLEASE HELP ME NEVER BE DISTRACTED FROM FOCUSING ON MY SPOUSE. BY YOUR GRACE AND IN YOUR POWER, MAY I FIND JOY IN MY SPOUSE'S BODY ALONE.

LOVE IN ACTION

1. Talk about any new insight into your sexual relationship this devotional offers. Pray about any issue it raises for the two of you. Dedicate yourselves anew to God and to each other.

2. Wives, on your own, spend a few minutes honestly evaluating whether you are making yourself a willing and available partner to your husband. Husbands, are you training your eyes only on your wife, or do you allow yourself that second glance?

Tender, well-regulated, domestic affection is the best defense against the vagrant desires of unlawful passion.
CHARLES BRIDGES

A PUZZLING DESIGN

Let him kiss me with the kisses of his mouth—
For your love is better than wine.

SONG OF SOLOMON 1:2

MICROWAVES AND CROCKPOTS . . . You've undoubtedly heard the analogy: men's sexual energies are up to temperature pretty much immediately, like a microwave warming a piece of pizza in twenty seconds; whereas, a woman's sexual temperature rises more slowly, like the crockpot that takes eight hours to cook a chicken.

And the differences don't stop there. What gets a man's temperature up can be a simple visual. What makes a woman's temperature rise is more complex. She wants to connect emotionally with her man. Feeling heard by him is key to her feeling loved. Many women want to be romanced beforehand, and many long to linger in his arms afterward.

When a woman has a man's attention—when he is truly interested in her, when he is approaching her heart instead of just her body—she will warm up for physical closeness.

That process can be short-circuited, though, if she spends too much time in the fantasy world of romance novels, soap operas, "chick flick" movies . . . you name it. Just as husbands are to train their eyes on their wife, wives are to keep their heart focused on their man—not on the dashing-but-completely-imaginary hero of the novel or the bad-boy leading man in the soap opera or movie.

Another warning to wives: don't allow your emotional needs to be completely met by girlfriends or the kids. God designed a married couple to be close in heart as well as body.

Which brings us back to microwaves and crockpots. Hang in there! The effort to elevate each other's temperatures in their proper time is worth the reward when that timer dings!

> LORD, YOUR DESIGN FOR MARRIAGE IS SO WONDERFUL.
> BUT IN MANY WAYS, MEN AND WOMEN SEEM SO OPPOSITE,
> AND THE MARRIAGE BED CERTAINLY BRINGS UP A KEY
> DIFFERENCE. LORD, WE THANK YOU FOR THE GIFT OF
> PHYSICAL INTIMACY, AND WE TRUST THAT YOU WILL HELP
> US LIVE OUT THIS BEAUTIFUL ASPECT OF OUR MARRIAGE TO
> YOUR GLORY.

Marriage doth signify merry-age.

HENRY SMITH

LOVE IN ACTION

1. Talk together about microwaves and crockpots and finding a balance in the bedroom. What can you do to be sensitive to each other's different warm-up times?

2. Now think for a bit on your own. Wives, what can you do to start warming up the crockpot before you close the bedroom door? Husbands, are you paying attention to your wife? Do you ask her to share her thoughts and feelings? When she does, what do you do to show her you're listening and you care?

NO ANGER
AFTER **SUNDOWN**

"Be angry, and do not sin": do not let the sun go down on your wrath, nor give place to the devil.

EPHESIANS 4:26–27

S OMETIMES IT'S A SLOW simmer.

Sometimes, the silent treatment.

And then there's the volcanic explosion.

Perhaps rarest of all is the rational, if not passionate, discussion. What's your default mode when you're angry at your spouse? Are you guided by the "old" self or the "new" creation in Christ?

Anger in and of itself is not sin. Jesus Himself got angry at the Pharisees and moneychangers in His Father's house (Matthew 21:12): His was a righteous anger. Our anger can be righteous when we react to people being abused or God's name slandered, but it is probably a fair statement to say that when we get angry at our spouse, it is rarely righteous.

Our anger usually does not stem from zeal to honor God's name, but rather from a deep-seated desire to please ourselves. And when anyone (even our spouse) gets in the way of us getting what we want—we get mad. We may feel jealous, resentful, or offended, but the root problem for most of our anger is selfishness. "For where envy and self-seeking exist, confusion and every evil thing are there" (James 3:16).

Regardless of the cause of our anger, today's verse is a great and biblical principle: don't let the day end without repenting of our anger and making peace with each other. Following that principle is key to not providing Satan with a foothold in our hearts or our marriage.

> LORD, I TOTALLY UNDERSTAND THE VALUE OF THAT
> SIMPLE, BUT NOT-ALWAYS-EASY-TO-FOLLOW RULE.
> PLEASE TEACH ME HOW TO DEAL WITH MY ANGER
> IN A DYING-TO-SELF, CHRISTLIKE WAY—AND HELP
> ME TO BE GRACIOUS WHEN MY SPOUSE REPENTS OF
> BEING ANGRY WITH ME AND TRIES TO MAKE PEACE.

No matter how just your words may be, you ruin everything when you speak with anger.
JOHN CHRYSOSTOM

LOVE IN ACTION

1. Choose your timing wisely. The heat of a fiery moment is probably not the best time to talk about anger management. Come up with a plan for making peace with your spouse before your day marked by anger ends.

2. In some quiet moments with the Lord, identify your favorite or default mode of being angry. What signs, subtle or otherwise, do you give your spouse that you're not happy? What would be a better approach to dealing with your anger?

NOT JUST *WITH*—BUT *FOR*, TOO!

Pray for one another, that you may be healed.
The effective, fervent prayer of a righteous man avails much.

JAMES 5:16

OKAY, SO THE TITLE of this devotional is a little tricky . . . just as the topic can be for many of us . . . .

Speaking through the apostle Paul, God gave us the general command to "pray without ceasing" (1 Thessalonians 5:17). And in James 5:16, we get the more specific call to pray for one another. Applied to our marriage, we are to pray not just *with* our spouse, but we are also to pray *for* him or her. After all, who on the planet is more aware of your spouse's needs, concerns, heartaches, and dreams?

Before you close this book, wanting to skip the guilt trip, know that our prayer life can be minimal to pretty much nonexistent at times. We are all sharpening our "pray without ceasing" skills. As we do, we would be wise to pray those along-the-way, through-the-course-of-your-day prayers for our spouse.

When a husband thinks of his wife, how about praying that God will give her the grace to get the day's tasks done, whether she spends her day in an office, at home, or a little of both—and pray for her spiritual growth. When a wife thinks of her husband, may she ask God to give him the wisdom and strength he needs for the projects of his day—and pray for his purity.

Like anything we do, the more we do it, the more easily it comes to us. So challenge yourself to "pray [more] continually"—and then watch God work in your heart and in the people and circumstances around you.

> LORD GOD, FORGIVE ME FOR TAKING FOR GRANTED THE
> AMAZING PRIVILEGE I HAVE OF COMING BEFORE YOUR
> THRONE, ANYTIME, DAY OR NIGHT. PLEASE WORK IN
> MY HEART THAT I MIGHT BE A MORE FAITHFUL PRAYER
> WARRIOR WITH AND FOR MY SPOUSE.

LOVE IN ACTION

1. Talk about your prayer times together. What could you do to make them richer— or to make them happen at all even just two or three times a week?

2. What everyday, very present object or recurring event might remind you to pray for your spouse? Maybe a glance at your watch or the ring of your cell might prompt a quick prayer for him or her.

Pray often rather than very long at a time. It is hard to be very long in prayer, and not slacken in our affections.
WILLIAM
GURNALL

STILL THE BEST POLICY

Do not lie to one another,
since you have put off the old man with his deeds.

COLOSSIANS 3:9

I T'S NOT EASY TO establish. Doing so takes time; the process can't be rushed. It may take much effort on your part—and it may require the other person to take a step of faith. Yet, it can be destroyed in an instant, sometimes irreparably. We're talking about trust, an essential cornerstone in a strong marriage.

Trust is based on the counter-cultural and unnatural skill of honesty. Our lies start when we're young, and as we grow, most of us become not only quite adept at lying, but we rise to the sister skills of rationalizing our lies as well as telling only partial truths. But God's standard for a marriage—for a life—that honors Him is clear: "Do not lie to one another." We must tell the whole truth at all times; Scripture doesn't make any exceptions.

The apostle Paul explained that since we are no longer the old creation we used to be, we are not to be liars. Reborn in Christ Jesus, we are new creations and, therefore, we are to put an end to the sinful deeds that came so easily before we were alive in Jesus. Furthermore, we are never to let our pride keep us from being honest, because your spouse and, even more importantly, your Lord deserve your complete honesty.

As with all of God's commands, obedience brings blessing: your marriage will be a safe place, and your intimacy will be genuine.

> Thank You, Lord, that You are a God of truth. Thank You that You are worthy of my complete trust. You do what You say You will do, and there is nothing untrue or inconsistent in You. And thank You that You can help me stand strong as a person of integrity—and please do so.

LOVE IN ACTION

1. In some quiet minutes with the Lord, renew your commitment to be honest in little things as well as big things. Ask Him to show you where you have failed to live up to that standard . . . what you need to confess to Him . . . and whose forgiveness you need to ask—and then do it. God will be with you as you untangle any relational knots, and He will enable you to become a more honest individual.

2. Talk together about why honesty is the best policy, what makes it hard to live by that policy, and how you can help each other be people of complete integrity.

FEARLESS FOR GOD

The LORD is my light and my salvation;
Whom shall I fear?
The LORD is the strength of my life;
Of whom shall I be afraid?

PSALM 27:1

WERE YOU EVER AFRAID that you'd never meet Mr. Wonderful or Miss Right? Then, when he came riding up on his white horse, did you fear that he might not recognize you or may not want you as the girl of his dreams? Or when she caught your eye in the crowded room, did you fear that she might not recognize or want you as her prince who had finally come?

We all have fears, and in this fallen world, many of those fears are all too grounded in reality. People get terminal illnesses and incurable diseases. Car accidents rob families of a parent . . . or a child . . . or both. The loss of a job or a business is often based in economic realities beyond our control.

The temptation to fear can come from many fronts, but a common fear is one we may not often consider: the fear of rejection. It hurts when someone rejects our efforts to reach out with love. And this fear often manifests itself in our steps to avoid sharing the gospel.

God calls us to boldly proclaim the truth about our sinfulness and the good news of Jesus' death as payment for that sin—but what will people think of us if we tell them? Will they think less of our intellectual abilities? What if our faith costs us a promotion? What if...?

Regardless of consequences, we should take great joy in communicating the eternal hope we have in Jesus. And we can take great comfort that, as we share this hope, God—who cares for the sparrows—will care for us as well. After all, we are more valuable to God than many sparrows (Matthew 10:31).

So instead of fearing man's rejection, let's courageously speak the truth in love. And as you and your spouse commit to the common goal of sharing the gospel, you will grow closer in your marriage as well.

> LORD GOD, YOU KNOW OUR HEARTS; YOU KNOW OUR FEARS. HELP US LET GO OF THOSE FEARS THAT KEEP US FROM BOLDLY WITNESSING FOR YOU.

Our help is in the name of the Lord, but our fears are in the name of man.
WILLIAM GREENHILL

LOVE IN ACTION

1. What fears do you struggle with? What about your spouse? What can you do to help each other deal with those fears?

2. Talk about what your life would look like if you were fearless-of-men, strong-in-the-Lord witnesses for God Almighty. What practical step can you take toward becoming that kind of light for the Lord?

IT'S ALL IN THE DELIVERY

There is one who speaks rashly like the thrusts of a sword,
but the tongue of the wise brings healing.

PROVERBS 12:18 NASB

* "There's a shock. You overdrew the checking account . . . again."
* "Now I'll be late for work. Why is it that every time you drive my car you bring it back with no gas?"
* "Same old, same old. I can't walk through the bedroom without tripping over your dirty clothes. It's called a hamper—you should meet it sometime."
* "I come home and every light in the house is on. Does it ever dawn on you that electricity costs money?"

THERE ARE SEEMINGLY COUNTLESS verses in the Bible dealing with the hurt we can cause with our speech, and so often it is not *what* we say, but *how* we say it. In marriage we can all probably point to times that we have made valid requests or truthful statements to our spouse, but—because of our rash choice of words—the messenger got in the way in the message. Hard-to-hear truth spoken in love is always better than hard-to-hear truth spoken critically or impatiently.

How's your delivery?

> JESUS, YOU SPOKE TRUTH BOLDLY WHEN YOU WALKED THIS EARTH. YOU HELPED US UNDERSTAND THAT WE ARE SINNERS IN NEED OF A SAVIOR AND THAT YOU ARE THAT SAVIOR. YOURS WAS A HARD TRUTH TO ACCEPT, BUT THAT TRUTH WAS A GIFT OF LOVE. TEACH US TO SPEAK OUR WORDS, ESPECIALLY TO EACH OTHER, WITH A HEART OF LOVE, NOT WITH A DESIRE TO HURT OR PUT DOWN. HELP US TO SPEAK AS WE WOULD WANT TO BE SPOKEN TO.

LOVE IN ACTION

1. What is a better delivery of the same messages given in the sample scenarios? Why are those alternatives a better or more effective approach?

2. On your own, ask God to help you think of new ways to respond to truth in love when it is spoken with a less-than-loving delivery. Make a list and practice saying your ideas. Then, when the next opportunity for confrontation arises, put your new response into action.

All our words ought to be filled with true sweetness and grace; and this will be so if we mingle the useful with the sweet.
JOHN CALVIN

Aaaaargh!!!

What I will to do, that I do not practice; but what I hate, that I do . . . . For the good that I will to do, I do not do; but the evil I will not to do, that I practice.

ROMANS 7:15, 19

O YOU FEEL THE apostle Paul's pain? Of course you do!

* You promised to fix the vacuum first thing Saturday morning, but it's 10:45 and you're still sleeping.
* You want to be patient with the kids, but you keep raising your voice at them.
* You committed to pray for your spouse. You did it for the first two days, but now you haven't for the last two weeks.

We do what we don't want to do. We don't do what we do want to do.

It's a truth we need to remember when it's our turn to forgive our spouse for doing the very thing she doesn't want to do, or for not doing the very thing he wants to do.

Two sinners trying to live together . . . Two sinners being used by the Lord to refine each other's character and to grow their faith in Him . . . Sparks can fly. Words are spoken that we wish we could take back. Certain actions go undone, and we wish we could rewind the clock—and the reverse is equally and perhaps more painfully true. *Why did I do that? What was I thinking?*

Two sinners trying to live together . . . and by God's grace they will know the joy of His blessing and of each other's companionship.

> LORD GOD, AS IF EVERY DAY ISN'T REMINDER ENOUGH
> THAT I NEED YOUR GRACE IN MY LIFE—THAT WE NEED
> YOUR GRACE IN OUR MARRIAGE—THE WORDS OF PAUL
> DRIVE THAT TRUTH HOME TODAY. PLEASE GIVE US THE
> GRACE TO LOVE EACH OTHER, AS WELL AS THE GRACE TO
> FORGIVE EACH OTHER WHEN WE FALL SHORT OF BEING
> THE PEOPLE WE WANT TO BE.

Think of the guilt of sin, that you may be humbled. Think of the power of sin, that you may seek strength against it. Think not of the matter of sin . . . lest you be more and more entangled.

JOHN OWEN

LOVE IN ACTION

1. Take turns answering this question: What is one of the greatest moments of receiving grace that you have experienced in your marriage?

2. Spend some time praying together. Thank your heavenly Father for making His grace more real through your spouse. Then pray about a specific example of "what I hate, that I do" that you would like, by God's strength, to overcome for the good of your marriage.

BREAK MY HEART, LORD

You do not desire sacrifice,
or else I would give it;
You do not delight in burnt offering.
The sacrifices of God are a broken spirit,
A broken and a contrite heart—
These, O God, You will not despise.

PSALM 51:16–17

WHEN WE TRUST OUR heart to another, it can get broken. When we entrust our broken heart to the Lord, it can be an offering He will not despise.

And a heart broken by the recognition of our sin is the kind of heart the psalmist, David, is referring to here. David definitely recognized his sin: adultery and murder are hard to miss!

God established the Old Testament sacrificial system to point His children to His gracious mercy. But Israel started trusting the sacrifices to save them, rather than the God receiving those sacrifices. David understood that God was not looking only for outward reform, but that He was in the business of transforming people inwardly. David also understood that he was a wretched sinner with nothing good to offer God. He was truly a broken man who could only appeal to God's mercy and grace.

God wants us to go to Him empty-handed and acknowledging that we are sinners with a debt we can never pay off on our own. God is the only One who can forgive our sin. And there are few things that bring us nose-to-nose with our sin, like marriage.

So cry out to God to forgive your sins. He will not, as David proclaimed, reject or despise a person whose heart is truly broken and contrite.

> LORD, SHOW ME THE SIN I'M SO COMFORTABLE WITH THAT I DON'T EVEN SEE IT ANYMORE . . . AND ANY SIN AGAINST MY SPOUSE THAT I'M TOO PRIDEFUL TO ACKNOWLEDGE. PLEASE FORGIVE ME FOR ALL OF THESE, LORD, AND PLEASE WASH ME WHITER THAN SNOW.

Other things may be the worse for breaking, yet a heart is never at the best till it be broken.
SIR RICHARD BAKER

LOVE IN ACTION

1. Looking first at the Lord, in His infinite perfection and glory, can help us see more clearly how He is God—and we are not. Together read one or more of the following passages, and may your time in God's Word prompt prayers of praise: 2 Samuel 22:32–34; Psalm 48:14; Psalm 62:7–8; Psalm 69:19–20; Psalm 116:5.

2. Sometimes it's good to confess our sin in writing and then burn that piece of paper. In addition to keeping others from reading what we wrote, the burning can vividly illustrate the truth that God removes our sin from us as far as the east is from the west (Psalm 103:12).

STRENGTH FOR THE ASKING

I will go in the strength of the Lord GOD;
I will make mention of Your righteousness, of Yours only.

PSALM 71:16

* He was sleep deprived and running a fever. Extra responsibilities at the office—a result of downsizing—were weighing heavily. And he was very aware of the significance of this assignment; yet, he nailed the sales presentation.
* She was awaiting the results of her daughter's MRI. Even though she felt she had a message prepared, how could she possibly focus enough to lecture at women's Bible study? But she spoke . . . and lives were changed.

IT MAY SOUND LIKE false humility when you don't take credit for what you've just accomplished, but such experiences—those times when you are able to accomplish something and you *know* it wasn't in your power—are an amazing reality.

We truly are sinners saved by God's grace alone, and the only righteousness we can speak of having is the imputed righteousness of Jesus Christ. So obviously we have nothing to brag about in and of ourselves, and being mindful of this truth should lead us to depend on the Lord daily.

And dependence on God, on His strength, is key to having a marriage that blesses us and glorifies Him. Only by relying on His strength can we truly die to self and serve our spouse. Only by relying on God's strength can we come nearer to experiencing all that He intends marriage to be. And that strength is ours for the asking.

THAT'S A PRETTY GOOD DEAL, LORD, THAT I CAN TURN
TO YOU FOR STRENGTH TO DO WHATEVER YOU CALL ME
TO DO, IN ANY AND EVERY ASPECT OF MY LIFE. KEEP
ME MINDFUL OF MY NEED FOR YOU SO THAT, IN YOUR
STRENGTH, I CAN BE THE HUSBAND OR WIFE YOU CALL
ME TO BE.

LOVE IN ACTION

1. Together, think back over your marriage, especially about the tougher days. When did God give one or both of you the strength to do something that you needed to do to benefit the relationship? Reflect on His faithful provision and be encouraged.

2. What do you need to do for your marriage that you simply can't do by your own power? Having realized that fact, what will be your next step?

In our own strength we must fall; but, when we hear the voice which saith, "Go in this thy might," we may advance without fear.
CHARLES SPURGEON

REST FOR YOUR SOUL

There remains therefore a rest for the people of God.
HEBREWS 4:9

* Are you trying to earn God's love rather than trusting in His grace?
* Are you a slave to performance Christianity?
* Are you trying to control every aspect of your life—or your spouse's?

WHEN YOU CATCH YOURSELF trying to live out your faith in your own flesh and in your own power (and we all do it), then take a deep breath and think about these words from Jesus:

Come to me, all you who are weary and burdened, and I will give you rest. Take my yoke upon you and learn from me, for I am gentle and humble in heart, and you will find rest for your souls. For my yoke is easy and my burden is light. (Matthew 11:28–30 NIV)

Make Jesus the resting place for your soul, for your marriage. Trust Him to guide and empower, trust in His plans for your future, and simply trust in His mercy and grace. He will be faithful to give you the peace and calm that you need in this chaotic and demanding world.

LORD, I WOULD LOVE FOR TRUST IN YOU TO REPLACE MY WORRY. I WOULD LOVE FOR PEACE IN YOU TO REPLACE MY MISGUIDED EFFORTS TO LIVE MY CHRISTIAN WALK IN MY OWN STRENGTH. PLEASE SHOW ME AREAS IN MY LIFE THAT I HAVE NOT COMPLETELY TURNED OVER TO YOU. PLEASE HELP ME TO COME INTO THE PEACE OF YOUR PRESENCE AND TO KNOW YOUR REST.

Entering the rest of God is the ceasing from self-effort, and the yielding up oneself in the full surrender of faith to God's working.
ANDREW MURRAY

LOVE IN ACTION

1. Talk together about what you can do as a couple to let trust replace worry.

2. In what ways are you trying to live life by your own strength rather than resting in the Lord? Are there any areas of life that you haven't, but want to turn completely over to Him? Talk to Him about it in prayer.

BEARING THE
FRUIT OF THE SPIRIT

*The fruit of the Spirit is love, joy, peace,
longsuffering, kindness, goodness, faithfulness, gentleness,
self-control. Against such there is no law.*

GALATIANS 5:22–23

PLOWING, SOWING, WATERING, WEEDING—FRUIT doesn't just appear automatically! The farmer works day and night with all diligence to do his part, so that, if the Lord wills, fruit will grow.

The same is true regarding the fruit of the Spirit: we do what we know to do (Bible study, prayer, worship, service, fellowship with other believers, and so on), and as the Lord wills, we will grow in our Christlikeness.

In the Bible, the fruit of the Spirit are the outward results of the inward transformation Christ has done in our lives. And the more we grow in Him, the more our lives will be manifesting these traits.

The fruit of the Spirit are:

* *Love*—having the kind of affection that leads to your willingness to sacrifice yourself.
* *Joy*—feeling glad in spite of your circumstances and because of God's unchanging promises.
* *Peace*—possessing a calm confidence because of your relationship with and your surrender to the Lord.
* *Longsuffering*—having the patience to accept and endure difficult situations for long periods without losing hope.

* *Kindness*—showing genuine concern for others.
* *Goodness*—having moral and spiritual excellence.
* *Faithfulness*—being loyal and trustworthy.
* *Gentleness*—using soft and tender words and actions.
* *Self-control*—restraining yourself in all areas of your life.

What's *not* to like about living with a person like that?! By God's power, you can be that kind of person!

> LORD, I WANT TO BE A BLESSING TO THE PERSON YOU ENTRUSTED TO ME AS A LIFE PARTNER. PLEASE KEEP ME WILLING TO DIE TO SELF AND DISCIPLINED IN MY EFFORTS TO PUT MYSELF IN YOUR TRANSFORMING PRESENCE. MAY YOU BE GLORIFIED IN MY LIFE AS THE FRUIT OF YOUR SPIRIT APPEARS.

LOVE IN ACTION

1. The fruit of God's Spirit is evident in Jesus in every scene of his life. Pick a gospel and spend a couple weeks reading through this account of Jesus' life. Note which fruit you see—*love, joy, peace, longsuffering, kindness, goodness, faithfulness, gentleness, self-control*—in any given scene.

2. Think about the Galatians 5 list of the Spirit's fruit. Why do you think they're in that particular order? What ideas do you have about the interrelationships of the nine?

Do not confound work and fruit. There may be a good deal of work for Christ that is not the fruit of the heavenly Vine.
ANDREW
MURRAY

WORK AS WORSHIP

Whatever you do, do it heartily, as to the Lord and not to men.

COLOSSIANS 3:23

W E'VE BOTH WORKED HARD today" is a good starting point when two tired people come together and their evening begins.

Maybe both of you are in the marketplace: yes, you worked hard. Maybe you work for yourself or maybe you volunteer your time and energy: yes, you worked hard. Maybe one of you is home with the kids: yes, you worked hard.

God blesses hard work, whether your work is done in the marketplace or at home, for a paycheck or as community service. And when we work hard—which includes getting to work on time and working with impeccable integrity—we honor the Lord.

The Puritans were the finest craftsmen of their day. So excellent was their work that kings and queens, dukes and duchesses, wanted their goods. Why were the Puritans' standards so high? Because they understood that, whatever they were doing, in the woodshop or in the sanctuary, they were to glorify the Lord. When the Puritans worked hard in order to honor the Lord, He blessed their efforts.

As we learn to be more diligent in our daily work habits, we just might find this attitude becomes contagious to all areas of our life. Let's work *heartily* in our spiritual disciplines, in our serving of others, in our being a more bold witness for Christ, and most definitely let's work hard in our marriage. And let's do it all *"as to the Lord."*

> LORD, THIS PERSPECTIVE ON WORK GIVES VALUE TO THE
> MUNDANE ASPECTS OF WHAT OUR DAYS HOLD. YOU ARE INDEED
> EMMANUEL, "GOD WITH US," AND MAY WE REMEMBER THAT
> AS WE GO ABOUT OUR DAILY BUSINESS, WHEREVER IT TAKES
> US. MAY OUR AWARENESS OF YOUR PRESENCE MAKE ALL THAT
> WE DO AN ACT OF WORSHIP.

I dare appeal to every one's experience, whether they find not more inward peace and satisfaction when their day has been diligently employed in their proper callings, than when it has been trifled away in sloth and folly.
RICHARD STEELE

LOVE IN ACTION

1. Take a break from work and go on a lunch date together. Talk specifically about what you appreciate about the work the other person does for the benefit of the marriage, the family, the home. And try to make it a regular habit to speak such words of appreciation.

2. What keeps you from giving your all to the work you do? What can you do to counter those forces and/or overcome those obstacles? Who, if anyone, might help you do so?

YOUR PREFERENCE?

A good name is to be chosen rather than great riches,
loving favor rather than silver and gold.

PROVERBS 22:1

WHAT DOES YOUR CHECKBOOK register reveal about what's really important to you?

In the privacy of your own mind, how many minutes in a day do you spend thinking about money?

Whether we like it or not, statistics tell us that the number one reason people divorce is . . . money. So with respect to encouraging God's best in our marriage, today's verse is fair warning not to make money too high a priority in our lives.

But it's so hard not to! Everything costs money—more and more of it with each passing year. Standard of living prices rise while our income levels stay the same or decrease. Add to that a few unexpected emergencies—the washing machine dies, an illness strikes—and you're wondering how you're going to pay the bills for the next month.

And, complicating matters, we have a hard time differentiating between needs and wants. Stores constantly claim "new" and "better" products that we can't live without. Catalogs fill our mail boxes with products we didn't know we needed until opening their pages. Television ads bombard us with the line "Buy it now, and we'll throw in a second one for free!" We get so distracted by saving money for our own personal pleasures, we forget that we are called to give to others . . . to be a blessing to those around us.

So what's the answer? We must have our eyes focused on the Giver.

Everything we have belongs to God, and He should be the focus of our life. If you are more passionate about pursuing Jesus and your spouse than you are pursuing wealth, then—simply put—you are choosing wisely.

> LORD GOD, I WANT YOU TO BE LORD OF MY LIFE.
> FORGIVE ME FOR THE WAYS I'VE LET MONEY BECOME
> A GOD, SOMETHING THAT'S ALL TOO IMPORTANT, EVEN
> ALL-CONSUMING AT TIMES. HELP ME STAND STRONG
> AND CHOOSE A GREAT NAME—"CHILD OF GOD!"—
> INSTEAD OF GREAT RICHES.

People may have money, and yet not love it; but, if they love it inordinately, it will push them on to all evil.
MATTHEW HENRY

LOVE IN ACTION

1. No more being rhetorical: What *does* your checkbook register reveal about your priorities? Do the ways you spend your finances accurately reflect your priorities? Do the ways you spend your money show that the Lord and your marriage is a priority?

2. Together, brainstorm what the two of you can do to weaken money's grip on you. If you're not regularly giving to the church, perhaps you can start. Or maybe you can sponsor a child through a reputable ministry or make an anonymous monetary gift to someone you know is in need. As the saying goes, "Give until it hurts—and then keep giving until it stops hurting."

MY FREEDOM—YOUR STUMBLING BLOCK

Beware lest somehow this liberty of yours
become a stumbling block to those who are weak.

I CORINTHIANS 8:9

TWO THOUSAND YEARS AGO when the church was young, some of the potential stumbling blocks were something like this:

* Are followers of Jesus Christ free to eat non-kosher meat? Are they free to eat meat from an animal sacrificed on a pagan altar to an utterly false god?

Fast-forward several centuries, and the issues are very different:

* Are followers of Jesus Christ free to dance or go to movies? Are we free to sing praise songs in the sanctuary, or must we stick to the hymns?

Jesus has given us great freedom in our Christian life, but He also calls us to exercise those freedoms with sensitivity and care. If our freedom to do something violates another Christian's view—if that certain something would violate our brother or sister's conscience—then we are to abstain.

And the same is true in our marriage. As we seek to love our spouse, we must be wary of doing anything that would violate our spouse's conscience. Similarly, as you and your spouse seek to have your marriage shine God's light in this world, be wary of doing something that would violate the consciences of those around you.

Exercising your liberties at the expense of weaker believers is against the clear teaching of the Scriptures. Let's make sure we use our freedoms

---

in Christ for the good of His kingdom and His people. HOLY SPIRIT, PLEASE PRICK MY CONSCIENCE BEFORE I DO OR SAY ANYTHING THAT WOULD UNINTENTIONALLY CAUSE A BROTHER OR SISTER IN CHRIST TO STUMBLE—AND PLEASE GIVE ME GREAT WISDOM AND DISCERNMENT AS TO HOW TO USE THE FREEDOMS YOU HAVE GIVEN ME.

LOVE IN ACTION

1. Take a moment to consider the freedoms you have in Christ. As you do, ask yourself these questions: Does Scripture give any specific direction about this specific activity? Is this activity going to bring me or us closer to the Lord? Is this an activity I would want Jesus to see me doing?

2. Either together or on your own, reflect on a time when a believer's words or actions—though not expressly sinful—may have caused you to stumble. Describe how you eventually resolved the matter in your own mind and conscience.

The conscience is not to be healed if it be not wounded.
WILLIAM PERKINS

COMPASSION AT HOME

Jesus wept.

JOHN 11:35

SOMETIMES THERE JUST AREN'T words for a difficult or sad situation. Sometimes comfort may not come from what you say, but from your just being there. And sometimes there's no more loving statement of compassion than when tears are shared.

Jesus had learned that His friend Lazarus was sick. By the time He arrives at Lazarus' home, His friend is dead. Lazarus' sisters Mary and Martha are mourning the loss of their brother, others in the town are wailing in grief, and Jesus, feeling their sadness . . . weeps.

Jesus' example calls us to be people of compassion, and what better place to start than within our homes.

Sometimes we can be expressionless, stoic, and unfeeling—and we may think that these are good attributes—but Christ showed us that in its proper setting, expressing compassionate emotion is godly *and* appropriate. Though not always the case, men tend to struggle more with carrying this out.

On the other hand, sometimes we can be overly emotional—and we let our feelings overrule the truth and even our lives. Women tend to struggle more on this side of the spectrum.

Men, if your tendency is to be unemotional, remember God calls you to have a sensitive and tender heart toward your wife. Ladies, if you lean toward being highly emotional, remember God calls you to exhibit self-control—and that includes control over your feelings.

The key, as with so much of our Christian lives, is to find that happy and healthy balance. Let's encourage each other to share our feelings, but let's also encourage each other to keep our emotions in line with the truth of God's Word.

Above all, let's all continually look to Jesus for guidance and His example.

> IT IS AMAZING TO CONSIDER THAT THE GOD OF THE UNIVERSE HAS COMPASSION FOR ME, FOR I AM MADE OF DUST. IT IS HUMBLING TO REALIZE THAT, AS YOU OVERSEE THE UNFOLDING OF HISTORY, YOU CARE SO DEEPLY ABOUT ME. THANK YOU FOR KNOWING ME AND LOVING ME, LORD GOD. HELP ME TO LOVE MY SPOUSE WITH THAT SAME KIND OF COMPASSIONATE LOVE.

LOVE IN ACTION

1. Think about the years you've shared, even the time before you were married. Now each of you tell your spouse of a time when they blessed you with the gift of compassion. Use this time to affirm your spouse and learn of any ways you can be more sensitive to your spouse's feelings.

2. What is something that may be keeping you from extending compassion to your spouse? Ask God to show you—and to help you become more compassionate toward him or her.

It is commendable in men to be compassionate, and to join with friends in their sorrows.
GEORGE HUTCHESON

SPECIAL IN GOD'S EYES

*You are a chosen generation, a royal priesthood, a holy nation,
His own special people, that you may proclaim the praises of Him
who called you out of darkness into His marvelous light.*

I PETER 2:9

REMEMBER THE FEELING THAT came with being chosen for the baseball team when you were in elementary school?

Or chosen to dance when you were celebrating the big victory after the high school football game?

Remember being chosen when he asked you to marry him, or when she said yes?

It's nice to be chosen for something because of our polished skills, our charming personality, our dashing looks, or even our godly character. But think about it: In God's eyes, there was *nothing* polished, charming, dashing, or godly about us—yet He still chose us to be His children. Out of His simple and good pleasure, He took undeserving, sinful people and, by His grace, made us His holy nation.

Chosen . . . not because of anything we do, but because of what Jesus Christ has already done. But there it is, in black and white, that you and I are "a chosen generation . . . [God's] own special people."

Let these words also remind you that your spouse is among God's chosen ones. Are you treating each other as such? You've been chosen to partner with a precious, God-crafted human being for life. May that truth prompt words of encouragement and thanksgiving for your spouse and words of praise for God!

LORD GOD, THANK YOU FOR CHOOSING ME—FOR CALLING ME
OUT OF DARKNESS TO BE YOUR CHILD. TEACH ME, SHOW ME,
HOW TO CONVEY MY APPRECIATION FOR MY SPOUSE, THE ONE
I CHOSE TO BE MY LIFELONG PARTNER. MORE IMPORTANTLY,
HELP ME TO ALWAYS REMEMBER THAT MY SPOUSE HAS BEEN
CHOSEN BY YOU AS WELL, AND TO LOVE THEM IN WAYS THAT
BRING LASTING PRAISE AND GLORY TO YOU.

The church (is) the gathering of God's children, where they can be helped and fed like babies and then, guided by her motherly care, grow up to manhood in maturity of faith.
JOHN CALVIN

LOVE IN ACTION

1. Catch a sunset with your spouse. Let the Lord's handiwork prompt you to marvel at His goodness and proclaim His praises. Also take a few minutes to praise and encourage your spouse. What do you especially appreciate about how he or she makes your life better? More complete? Let your spouse know some specifics.

2. Talk with the Lord about the amazing truth that He has chosen you to be His child. How does being chosen foster your sensitivity to people who are lonely? In front of whom does God want you to show Him praise so that they might know what it means to be chosen by Him?

ACTIONS SPEAK LOUDLY

With their mouth they show much love,
but their hearts pursue their own gain.

EZEKIEL 33:31

* You hear your name called, but your favorite team is on the five-yard
  line with a minute to go.
* The garage door goes up, but you really want to see who was the
  biggest loser.
* It wouldn't take long to pick up the dry cleaning, but you're really
  enjoying that cup of coffee.

TALK IS CHEAP. THAT'S as true in marriage as it is in the business
world, athletics, or any other realm of human activity. We all need
our actions to back our words. In fact, we need our actions to illustrate the truth of our words.

Telling your spouse "I love you" is wonderful—but it needs to be backed
by continual acts of dying to self.

"I'd be glad to help" needs to be translated into a helpful act.

"You matter to me" needs to be communicated by putting down the
paper and listening—really listening—even if you've heard it all before.

Actions do speak louder than words. So keep telling your spouse you
love him or her—but much more than that—show it!

> LORD, THANK YOU FOR THE BLESSING OF MY SPOUSE.
> FORGIVE ME FOR THE WAYS I MAKE HIM OR HER FEEL
> LESS THAN IMPORTANT. HELP ME TO CHANGE MY WAYS.
> ENABLE ME TO BE ALERT FOR OPPORTUNITIES TO LOVE
> WITH MY ACTIONS, NOT JUST MY WORDS.

LOVE IN ACTION

1. Ask your spouse which three acts of love are especially significant to them. Make a mental note of them and choose one to do this week.

2. Name something specific from today's devotional that challenged you. Act upon that challenge and strengthen your marriage.

At the day of Doom men shall be judged according to their fruits. It will not be said then, Did you believe? But, Were you Doers, or Talkers only?
JOHN BUNYAN

THINKING THE BEST

*Whatever things are true, whatever things are noble, whatever
things are just, whatever things are pure, whatever things are lovely,
whatever things are of good report, if there is any virtue and if there
is anything praiseworthy—meditate on these things.*

PHILIPPIANS 4:8

THEY SURROUND US . . . They are everywhere . . .
They are the non-stop messages from our noisy world that run
absolutely counter to God's Word and His standards. And all they
do is skew our perspectives, values, and contentment level.

If only our brains had a delete key!

Actually, if only our brain could be programmed like a computer, we
would do well to only feed it data that is . . .

* *True*—not false, inaccurate, or ungodly
* *Noble*—worthy of respect
* *Just*—in accordance with God's standards of holiness
* *Pure*—morally clean; undefiled
* *Lovely*—worthy of admiration; beautiful
* *Of good report*—highly thought of

Imagine how a mind filled with such virtuous and praiseworthy thoughts
would impact our words, our actions, and our way of thinking about our
spouse and our marriage. We would be less judgmental, more humble, less
worldly, more Christlike. If only we could hire a brain programmer.

We can't do that, but we *do* have God's Spirit within us to help us choose
to meditate on these good things!

> LORD GOD, I'M AMAZED BY THE THOUGHTS THAT
> SOMETIMES COME INTO MY MIND THAT DISHONOR
> YOU. I NEED YOUR SPIRIT TO HELP ME CLEAN UP
> AND CONTROL MY THOUGHT LIFE. SPIRIT, PLEASE
> HELP ME MEDITATE ON WHAT IS TRUE, NOBLE, JUST,
> PURE, LOVELY, OF GOOD REPORT, VIRTUOUS, AND
> PRAISEWORTHY. I KNOW I CAN'T DO IT WITHOUT YOU.

*Good works
do not make
a good man,
but a good
man does
good works.*
MARTIN
LUTHER

LOVE IN ACTION

1. Take a tour of your home. What magazines or books reflect the world's messages rather than the Lord's standards? Together, prayerfully consider removing those. Take the same sort of inventory of your TV-watching patterns. Which programs, if any, would you be better off not watching? And what will you *do*—not necessarily *watch*—instead?

2. As you sit quietly with the Lord, take your personal inventory a step further. What daydreams, fantasies, or common thought patterns would the Holy Spirit have you avoid for your own good? And what Scripture passages will you focus on and memorize instead? Find a handful and get started.

Worth the Wait

Wait on the LORD;
Be of good courage,
And He shall strengthen your heart;
Wait, I say, on the LORD!

PSALM 27:14

* Waiting at the airport for the flight that will reunite us . . .
* Waiting as the clock slowly ticks until we can go on our special
  date . . .

IT CAN BE HARD waiting for something fun and exciting to happen!
But how much harder is it when all we're waiting for is relief from
the pain or trial we're in?

We can feel like soldiers, side by side in the hole, just trying to get
through the barrage of enemy gunfire and hoping for reinforcements to
come.

During the difficult seasons of life, sometimes the *only* thing we can do
is wait on the Lord.

But be encouraged that our waiting is not in vain, as our loving Father
will not only give us strength to endure, but in His timing and in His way,
He will deliver us from whatever struggle we are in.

In His grace and mercy, God may bring relief quickly, and we can look
back with a smile and say, "That was a tough time. Thank You for bringing
us through that one, Lord!"

Other trials may not be that simple, and some may even last the rest of
our lives. But we can still take great comfort in knowing that not even our
worst trial will last forever because at some point our Savior will come, just
as He promised.

In our marriage as well as in our lives, we all have pain and suffering,
and at times it may seem like there's no end in sight. But, by the power of

the Holy Spirit, let's trust in God to give us strength and endurance. And let's always remember, whatever state we are in, this world is not our final home.

Come, Lord Jesus!

> LORD GOD, THANK YOU FOR REMINDING ME THAT EVEN THOUGH YOU ALLOW TRIALS, YOU ARE STILL A MERCIFUL, PROMISE-KEEPING GOD. PLEASE GIVE US STRENGTH TO GET THROUGH THESE TIMES, AND HELP US HAVE A GREATER ANTICIPATION OF SPENDING ETERNITY WITH YOU.

LOVE IN ACTION

1. What are you and your spouse waiting on God for right now? What can you do to help your spouse during this season?

2. When in your marriage have you had to wait on God? Encourage each other by reminding yourselves of His faithfulness and what was, in retrospect, clearly His perfect timing.

He who writes these scanty notes has himself found it so sweet, so reviving, so profitable to draw near to God, that on his own account he also feels bound to write, "Wait, I SAY, on the Lord."
CHARLES SPURGEON

BATTLING, BUT NOT CONDEMNED

There is therefore now no condemnation
to those who are in Christ Jesus,
who do not walk according to the flesh,
but according to the Spirit.

ROMANS 8:1

* I committed to losing thirty pounds, so why did I eat the entire carton of ice cream? I hate myself right now.
* We can barely pay our bills, but I still bought a new set of golf clubs. How could I be so selfish?
* I promised I would be more patient. I can't believe I just yelled at the kids again. I'm a horrible parent.

IT'S THE STRUGGLE WE all deal with. We so often do or say the wrong thing and equally often don't do or say the right thing. And instead of sincerely confessing it and moving on, we carry it, we drag it around like a ball and chain, and we continue to beat ourselves up over it.

Even though we are born anew in Christ Jesus, that new nature is encased in a body with all its bad habits and wrong thinking. This reality could be very discouraging, but look again at what the apostle Paul proclaimed immediately after he, too, bemoaned the struggle we have with our flesh. "There is . . . no condemnation," he rejoiced. Yes, we still struggle with sin, but the penalty for that sin—past, present, and future—was paid on the Cross.

Understanding God's forgiveness, Paul confidently declared that he "[forgets] those things which are behind and [reaches] forward to those things which are ahead" (Philippians 3:13). What a great example for us all.

In Christ, we have victory over our sins; we can never be condemned for them. What a wonderful reason to live in obedience to Jesus—out of gratitude for all that He has done for us!

> YOU KNOW THE BATTLE I FIGHT AGAINST MY FLESH, LORD!
> I THANK YOU THAT YOU WON'T CONDEMN ME ANYMORE,
> BUT I DO ASK THAT YOU WOULD HELP ME WIN THE BATTLE
> MORE OFTEN.

It is impossible for God Himself to find a flaw in the righteous position of any believer in the Lord Jesus Christ.
DONALD GREY BARNHOUSE

LOVE IN ACTION

1. Whether they happened ten years ago or ten minutes ago, are you holding onto any past failures? Confess them to the Lord and read Philippians 3:13. Then ask God to help you forget those things which are behind so that you may more joyfully serve Him as well as your spouse.

2. Commit Romans 8:1 to memory. And the next time you find yourself depressed over your sin, ask the Lord's forgiveness and say the verse out loud.

AN ATTITUDE OF GRATITUDE

Enter his gates with thanksgiving, and his courts with praise;
give thanks to him and praise his name.
For the LORD is good and his love endures forever;
his faithfulness continues through all generations.

PSALM 100:4–5 NIV

* She just doesn't appreciate all my sacrifices.
* He totally takes me for granted.
* The kids are so ungrateful for what all that we do for them.

WE ALL LIKE TO be thanked for what we do, but it's so easy to go through life and not show gratitude to the very ones we love the most.

So today is the day we give thanks! And let's start by giving thanks to our loving Father for all He is and all He has done for us. Here are five things to get you started.

Thank the Lord for . . .

* *Creating* you, your spouse, and all the beauty you enjoy in this world.
* *Forgiving* us for all the sins: past, present, and future.
* *Sanctifying* us and, by the power of the Holy Spirit, growing us to be more and more like Jesus.
* *Preserving* us and keeping us saved for all eternity.
* *Jesus Christ*, who lived a perfect life and died a painful death for us. Only because of what He has done can we have a relationship with You.

You can spend the rest of the day thanking Him if you like, but be sure to spend some time thanking your spouse for those little things he or she does for you!

As we grow to be more and more thankful, our home will be a happier place and our marriage will be a loud trumpet proclaiming the greatness of our awesome God!

> LORD GOD, LET US BE A COUPLE WHO REGULARLY GIVES YOU THANKS. AND PLEASE HELP US TO HAVE GROWING HEARTS OF GRATITUDE TOWARD EACH OTHER.

As the Lord loveth a cheerful giver, so likewise a cheerful thanksgiver.
JOHN BOYS

LOVE IN ACTION

1. Take a moment to thank God for three specific things He has done for you as a couple. Then take turns thanking your spouse for three specific things he or she has done for you. Finally, give each other a one-minute back rub.

2. Make a point this week to seek out a person (other than your spouse) whom you may have taken for granted—maybe a boss, a friend, or a pastor—and tell that person "Thank you!"

A WALK
DOWN **MEMORY LANE**

Remember His marvelous works which He has done,
His wonders and the judgments of His mouth.

1 CHRONICLES 16:12

THINK BACK OVER ALL the decisions you made to get you to the spot where you first met your spouse . . . Review in your mind God's work in your heart to prepare you to make a lifelong commitment . . .

List some of the amazing ways He has provided for you during your married years . . .

In David's song of thanksgiving, he calls the people of Israel to recall God's power and faithfulness in His covenants, His deliverance of them from Egypt, His forty years of provision in the wilderness, and even His marvelous act of creation (1 Chronicles 16:7–36).

Likewise, we do well to recall God's power and faithfulness in our life. Of course this side of the cross, the greatest demonstration of that divine goodness is the eternal sacrifice Jesus made for us. Yet a litany of God's goodness and grace continues in very personal ways as we look back over our journey through this life, our journey of faith.

So we can join in David's celebration: "Oh, give thanks to the LORD, for He is good! For His mercy endures forever" (1 Chronicles 16:34).

> LORD, YOU ARE GOOD! YOU BLESS US ABUNDANTLY
> WITH ALL THAT WE NEED AND MORE. YOU BLESS US
> WITH YOUR VERY PRESENCE THAT COMFORTS AND
> GUIDES, PROTECTS AND TRANSFORMS. THANK YOU
> FOR YOUR BLESSED PRESENCE IN OUR MARRIAGE.

LOVE IN ACTION

1. Writing a psalm is not a requirement and putting your words to music is definitely optional, but do take time together to list some good memories of God's workings that led the two of you to meet, date, and ultimately marry. Recount how God's faithfulness has prompted praise and added strength to your marriage bond. Be sure to include specific examples of how He has blessed your life together since you said, "I do."

2. Consider making a more permanent tribute to God's faithfulness. Some families gather smooth stones, a modern-day reflection of the stones our Old Testament forefathers set up to mark spots where God delivered them. The families write on each stone a phrase describing what God did, and then they date that event. A basket of stones is harder to miss than a piece of paper, but writing it on paper works as well!

There is no saint here who can out-believe God. God never out-promised Himself yet.
C. H. SPURGEON

GOD'S GOODNESS IN THE FLAMES

I have been young, and now am old;
Yet I have not seen the righteous forsaken,
Nor his descendants begging bread.

PSALM 37:25

CONSIDER THE SOURCE" IS always good advice. The *who* behind a statement can make its words staggeringly remarkable or utterly insignificant. In the case of Psalm 37:25, the *who* is an older David who, looking back on his life, marvels at God's goodness all his days.

Few have or will experience more of the dramatic highs and lows life has to offer than David. From heroic victories and his rise to king to the devastating loss of one son (2 Samuel 12:18) and the violent rebellion of another—eventually resulting in that son's death as well (2 Samuel 18:9)—David had "seen it all."

Much of David's suffering came as chastisement from the Lord—the consequences of his sin. Yet even in his darkest hour, he never lost sight of God's goodness. Even after a lifetime of difficulty, David could confidently proclaim this foundational truth: God is faithful to his children.

In marriage we may experience painful trials, devastating losses, and major setbacks. But even if much of our pain is caused by our own past sin, let's stand with David, "a man after God's own heart," think deeply on our loving God's faithfulness amidst the flames, and thank Him.

O LORD, FORGIVE US FOR OUR DISOBEDIENCE AND ALL THE TIMES WE STRAY FROM YOUR PATH. WE ASK THAT YOU WOULD HELP US WANDER LESS. HELP US ALSO BE VERY AWARE OF YOUR GOODNESS IN OUR LIVES. EVEN AMIDST OUR TRIALS, MAY WE GIVE YOU THE GLORY YOU DESERVE FOR THE BLESSINGS WE ENJOY—AND HELP US TO BE GOOD STEWARDS OF THOSE BLESSINGS, ESPECIALLY THE BLESSING OF MARRIAGE.

He is called the "Father of mercy," as who should say, He begets mercy, even a generation of mercies, from day to day.
THOMAS HOOKER

LOVE IN ACTION

1. Work together to make a list of God's acts of faithfulness to you as a couple. Think of times when you may have had little or experienced a prolonged trial, yet God continually provided.

2. When has God's discipline been evidence of His faithfulness to you? Reflect together how you grew individually and as a couple during those seasons.

TRUSTING YOUR
TRUSTWORTHY LORD

Trust in the LORD with all your heart,
And lean not on your own understanding;
In all your ways acknowledge Him,
And He shall direct your paths.

PROVERBS 3:5–6

FOUR-YEAR-OLD DANNY WAS STANDING at the edge of the pool. He'd never been so scared in his life. He had no inflatable armbands, no life vest, nothing. It was just Danny, the water, and Dad. Dad had never let him down before, but Danny was still terrified at the thought of drowning. Dad, who was patiently standing in the water with his arms stretched out, reaching forward, confidently encouraged his son, "It's OK, Danny, I'll catch you. Trust me."

Trust, in this context means putting your whole weight on something—and doing so with no backup, no plan B, if that something doesn't support you as you'd hoped it would.

Trusting God with your life means letting Him guide your steps and relying on Him to enable you to discern His instructions, obey His commands, and use you in His kingdom work. Will you always understand why He has you doing certain things or going in certain directions? No. If you did, your steps wouldn't require trust.

Now consider how you and your spouse are trusting (or not trusting) God. Maybe financial hardship or the death of a child has you both desperately clinging to Him. Maybe infidelity or the surfacing of past sexual trauma is requiring you to trust God more than ever to help you through. Will you always understand why He has allowed you to experience certain things, or why He has you going in certain directions? No. Or, once again, your steps wouldn't require trust.

The good news is, we aren't called to *blind* trust. Our God has proven His trustworthiness in His Word and reassures us of His love in our times of need. So when you spend time with Him, acknowledge His ways, relinquish your need to understand, and jump in with all your heart, He'll always catch you.

> I BELIEVE, LORD;
> HELP MY UNBELIEF.

LOVE IN ACTION

1. Take some time together to remember three ways God has shown you that He is completely, utterly, unswervingly trustworthy.

2. As gently as possible, husband, challenge your wife by bringing to her attention one area in which you think she may be anxious and not fully trusting God. Then let your wife do the same for you. Take a few moments to think through today's verse. Then pray together.

Let the will be kept in a quiet, subdued, cheerful readiness, to move, stay, retreat, turn to the right hand or to the left, at the Lord's bidding.
CHARLES BRIDGES

SHOUT, SHOUT, AND SHOUT **SOME MORE!**

*And they sang responsively, praising and giving thanks
to the LORD: "For He is good, for His mercy endures
forever toward Israel." Then all the people shouted with
a great shout, when they praised the LORD, because the
foundation of the house of the LORD was laid.*

EZRA 3:11

LOUD PEOPLE. LOUD PLACES. Go to any major sporting
event and that's what you'll find. Passion and excite-
ment, cheers and applause—all for the home team.

And the people of Israel were quite the home team. They
had banded together for the sole purpose of rebuilding the
temple. They counted it a great privilege to be involved, so
with willing hearts they sacrificed all they had for this worthy cause. When the foundation, the cornerstone, was finally
laid, there were great shouts of joy because the dream was becoming a reality (Ezra 3:8–13). What a time for celebration!

We too can experience this joy as we invest our time, tal-
ent, and resources in our local church and in our brothers
and sisters in Christ. As we pour our hearts into the lives of
our fellow believers, we can celebrate the fact that, like the
people of Israel, we are being used by God to help build His
kingdom.

And every day, as we commit ourselves to invest everything we have in our marriage, we too can shout for joy in

knowing that we are building upon the foundation of a sacred sacrament ordained and blessed by God Himself.

So start the applause, let out a cheer, and jump up and down if you want. Our Lord is great! And there's no better person on the planet to join you in shouting to the Lord than your spouse.

> FATHER, WE ARE HUMBLED THAT YOU USE US TO HELP BUILD YOUR KINGDOM. PLEASE HELP US POUR OUR WHOLE HEARTS INTO YOUR CHURCH, AS WELL AS INTO OUR BROTHERS AND SISTERS IN CHRIST. ABOVE ALL, WE PRAY THAT OUR LIVES WILL BE FILLED WITH JOY AS WE DEDICATE OURSELVES TOWARD THE MOST WORTHY CAUSE . . . OUR MARRIAGE.

There is no virtue in the Christian life which is not made radiant with joy; there is no circumstance and no occasion which is not illuminated with joy. A joyless life is not a Christian life, for joy is one constant recipe for Christian living.
WILLIAM
BARCLAY

LOVE IN ACTION

1. Open your Bibles and read Psalm 150. Write this great psalm down on paper. Then place it somewhere as a daily reminder to praise our wonderful Lord.

2. Give each other a kiss, then tell your spouse that there's no one you'd rather praise the Lord with. Husbands, you go first. Put it in your own words. Come on! Say it like you mean it!

My Shepherd | *The LORD is my Shepherd, I shall not want.*

PSALM 23:1

TALK ABOUT A TWENTY-FOUR-HOUR-A-DAY job—that is the life of a shepherd.

Sheep are very difficult animals. They need constant tending, and the shepherd's charge is to take care of the woolly creatures at all cost.

This is the picture that we are given in Psalm 23: the Lord is our shepherd, and we are His sheep.

As our Shepherd, He:
* protects us from evil.
* provides for our needs, both physical and spiritual.
* disciplines us when we go off the path.
* rules over us in love, and for our good.

As His sheep, we:
* follow Him.
* trust Him.
* belong to Him.
* are dependent upon Him.

Like sheep, left on our own we will stray and find ourselves in a world of trouble. We can all probably relate to hymn writer Robert Robinson's lament, "[I am] Prone to wander, Lord I feel it, prone to leave the God I love" from his classic "Come Thou Fount of Every Blessing." Or as Isaiah put it, "All we like sheep have gone astray, we have turned, every one, to his own way" (Isaiah 53:6). All of us are helpless, wandering sheep in need of a loving, caring, capable shepherd.

Thankfully, Psalm 23 is in present tense. We can know that our Lord, our Shepherd is watching, defending, correcting, and guiding us every step of our lives today.

In marriage we desperately need the love or our Shepherd to keep us safe and protected. So let's be careful not to wander from our Lord, because the closer we are to Him, the closer we will be to our spouse.

> OUR GOOD SHEPHERD, PLEASE HELP US BECOME MORE DEPENDENT ON YOU. HELP US NOT TO WANDER FROM YOU OR FROM EACH OTHER EMOTIONALLY OR PHYSICALLY. WE ARE THANKFUL THAT YOU WILL GROW US CLOSER TO EACH OTHER AS WE GROW CLOSER AND CLOSER TO YOU.

O come in therefore to Jesus Christ; let Him be now the Shepherd of thy soul.

JOHN DURANT

LOVE IN ACTION

1. During one of your quiet times in the next few weeks, read Psalm 23 and John 10:1–18. Note what a wonderful Shepherd we have in Jesus Christ.

2. Make a point to walk in the steps of the Good Shepherd. Together, seek out someone in need and extend His love to this person. Look for ways to help this person tangibly and be sure to notice the Lord's goodness made manifest in how He meets your needs.

CRIPPLED AND LAME

*"As for Mephibosheth," said the king, "he shall eat at my table
like one of the king's sons."*

2 SAMUEL 9:11

WHAT IF YOU WERE INVITED to dine with the President of the
United States?

Who would you tell? What would you wear? What would
you plan to talk about? Regardless of your political persuasion, imagine
your anticipation, your preparation, and perhaps your nerves as the evening
approached.

All that and more may be what Mephibosheth felt when he received
King David's invitation.

Mephibosheth was the grandson of Saul, Israel's first king. Saul, to put it
mildly, was not very nice. He continually sought to kill David, whom God
appointed to be king. When news came of the death of Saul and David
emerged as king, Saul's family fled. During their flee, Mephibosheth, still
a baby, was accidentally dropped by his nurse and was crippled for life. In
a flash, young Mephibosheth had gone from heir to the throne to handi-
capped fugitive.

Time passed and Mephibosheth grew. His painful past was a mere memory, until the day he received a notice: David had summoned him. "Why
is King David asking for me?" Mephibosheth must have wondered, *Is he
going to kill me?*

Well, David did not kill Mephibosheth. Instead, he invited the crippled man to eat at his table, and then he gave the order to restore to Mephibosheth all the land that had once belonged to his grandfather—and
David's former enemy—Saul.

What a picture of all that Christ does for us! We are not only crippled by our sin, but our sin has left us dead (Ephesians 2:1). "But because of his great love for us, God, who is rich in mercy, made us alive with Christ even when we were dead in transgressions" (Ephesians 2:4–5, NIV).

Jesus invites us into His kingdom and seats us at His table. He restores and heals our brokenness so that we are whole. What amazing grace and kindness!

> LORD GOD, MAY I NEVER FORGET HOW AMAZING IT IS THAT YOU HAVE INVITED ME TO YOUR TABLE—FOR ETERNITY! I WAS ENTIRELY CRIPPLED BY SIN, AND I STILL STUMBLE ALONG IN IT. YET YOU LOVE ME. MAY I NEVER FORGET WHAT THAT INVITATION COST YOU . . . THE LIFE OF YOUR PRECIOUS SON, MY SAVIOR, JESUS.

Trust the past to God's mercy, the present to God's love, and the future to God's providence.

ST. AUGUSTINE

LOVE IN ACTION

1. Take a few moments and read through 2 Samuel 9 together. Notice David's goodness to Mephibosheth and reflect on God's goodness to you.

2. Whom did God use to invite you to His table? If possible, write a brief note to one or two of the people instrumental in your naming Jesus as Savior and Lord.

A LOOK IN THE REARVIEW MIRROR

We . . . are being transformed into [Jesus'] likeness
with ever-increasing glory.

2 CORINTHIANS 3:18 NIV

"My, YOU'VE GROWN!" AND "You've gotten so tall!" are comments that tend to come from people who don't see the growing person very often. It's harder to note growth in ourselves or in those we see daily.

But that's the challenge today—to hold up a mirror to your spouse so that he or she can be encouraged by the growth in Christlikeness that you have noticed.

* Think back to your spouse before their conversion. Maybe you knew each other back then, or perhaps you've only heard the "before" story. Either way, point out three or four significant contrasts between that "before" and the ongoing "after."

* In past areas of your life you've probably been able to say with Paul, "What I hate, that I do . . . the evil I will not to do, that I practice" (Romans 7:15, 19). What hateful actions are you now doing less often?

* On the flip side, Paul's experience was undoubtedly like yours in this way as well: "What I will to do, that I do not practice . . . the good that I will to do, I do not do" (Romans 7:15, 19). What good acts are you now doing more often?

* Ask your spouse to identify and comment on any changes in heart, any growth in spiritual maturity, that he or she has noticed within himself or herself. Is worship more fulfilling? Is Bible study more appealing? Are you hungrier for solitude with the Lord and quiet time in His Word?

Spiritual growth doesn't make for a great science fair project, because subtle but significant growth is not always easy to measure. Nevertheless, the growth is real, and we need our brothers and sisters in Christ to point it out and encourage us. And there's no closer brother or sister than the person you married.

LORD, THANK YOU FOR TODAY'S REMINDERS THAT YOU ARE DOING YOUR TRANSFORMING WORK IN MY SPOUSE AND IN ME, MAKING US MORE LIKE JESUS, MORE THE PEOPLE YOU CREATED US TO BE.

LOVE IN ACTION

1. Summarize the discussion you just had with your spouse. Write some of these encouraging truths about the growth of this precious sibling-in-the-Lord so that he or she can have a more permanent record of it.

2. Now look again at the series of questions and let your spouse point out your spiritual growth. Thank God that He who has begun in you the good work of making you more like Christ will see it through to completion (Philippians 1:6).

Sanctification is the first fruit of the Spirit; it is heaven begun in the soul.
THOMAS WATSON

SHINE, BABY! SHINE!

*Let your light so shine before men, that they may see
your good works and glorify your Father in heaven.*

MATTHEW 5:16

T HE IMAGE WAS STRIKING. The Sunday school teacher turned off
all the lights, and the room was dark. Holding a hand up in front
of our own face, we couldn't count fingers. Then, standing in the
far corner, the teacher struck a single match. That one little light greatly
impacted the area right where the teacher stood, and that one little light
lightened the darkness throughout the entire room.

Jesus calls us to be lights of the world. We are to live in such a way that when
others watch us, they can clearly see the Lord working in and through us.

God puts all of us in different circumstances: maybe we work in an
office with a dozen co-workers, maybe we teach twenty students in a class-
room, maybe we head a company of a thousand employees, or maybe our
days our spent running the kids from school, to the dentist, then to practice, then home to make dinner. It doesn't matter what we do or how we
spend our days. Our job is simply to be a faithful light in whatever darkness
has been laid before us.

Like the tiny match, we sometimes may feel quite small and insignificant. Yet in the hands of our almighty God, even a tiny light can shine
exceedingly bright.

But let's first be sure we're God's light in our home and to our spouse.
We are to reflect His goodness to those persons closest to us, and our spouse
is at the top of that list.

> LORD, THANK YOU FOR THE MANY WAYS YOU INVOLVE US AND
> USE US IN YOUR KINGDOM WORK. PLEASE SHOW ME THE WAYS
> I CAN SHINE BRIGHTER FOR YOU—AND PLEASE GIVE ME THE
> COURAGE TO DO SO.

The Christian is a person who makes it easy for others to believe in God.
ROBERT M. MCCHEYNE

LOVE IN ACTION

1. Talk together about people who have been a light for Christ in your life, before and after you became a Christian. Encourage each other with an honest evaluation of the ways you both are God's light in the various circles in which He has placed you.

2. Ask God to show you what dark area in your community or place of employment He may be wanting you to shine His light. Be ready to obey!

King of Kings | *Our God is in heaven;*
He does whatever He pleases.

PSALM 115:3

MAYBE YOU HEARD IT when you were growing up. Maybe, if you're a parent, you've said it yourself: "Because I'm the dad!" or "Because I'm the mom!" These appeals to parental authority really do reflect the bottom line when it comes to the family hierarchy.

"Because I'm God—the One and Only, the King of kings, the Almighty Sovereign Lord!" clearly communicates divine authority when it comes to our relationship with our heavenly Father.

We serve a God who does not answer to anyone. Neither does He seek counsel before He makes a decision. Eternal in nature and infinite in wisdom, power, knowledge, and love, God is sovereign: He is in complete control of the electrons spinning around every atomic nucleus, as well as the stars sparkling in all the galaxies of this universe.

God limits Satan and sin, and He sustains His creation. Nothing little or big happens in this world—or in your life—unless God allows it. What a source of comfort this truth is! He has decreed all things that you are going through right now. He has overseen your past, He is overseeing your present, and He will see that your future plays out exactly as He, in His wisdom and love, wants it to. Nothing that you experience catches God off guard. What about those puzzling sources of struggle, loss, and pain? He allows and uses these situations for the good of His kingdom and for His glory.

So rest in God's sovereignty and don't worry about the future. It's in His mighty hands.

OUR LOVING FATHER, WE CERTAINLY WOULDN'T HAVE MUCH USE FOR A GOD WE COULD GET OUR FINITE MINDS AROUND AND WHOSE WAYS WE COULD TOTALLY UNDERSTAND. WE PRAISE YOU, OUR INFINITE KING OF KINGS AND SOVEREIGN LORD! WE DON'T ALWAYS UNDERSTAND WHY THINGS HAPPEN, BUT WE REST IN KNOWING THAT YOU ARE ALL LOVING, ALL WISE, ALL JUST, ALL POWERFUL, AND ALL GOOD.

LOVE IN ACTION

1. What current set of painful, puzzling, or difficult circumstances is calling you to trust God? Talk together about what He may want the two of you to learn from this experience.

2. What event in your life remains a vivid testimony of God's sovereign power and fatherly love for you? Reflect on that faith-building time right now.

There is no foundation for comfort in the enjoyments of this life, but in the assurance that a wise and good God governeth the world.
WILLIAM LAW

THE BIG-PICTURE **PERSPECTIVE**

For I know the thoughts that I think toward you, says the LORD,
thoughts of peace and not of evil, to give you a future and a hope.

JEREMIAH 29:11

WARS AND RUMORS OF WARS . . . Nation rising against nation . . . Famines, pestilence, earthquakes . . . Trade deficits and national debts . . . Job insecurity and personal debt . . . Physical illness and emotional overload . . . Challenges on both the kid-raising and the marriage-preserving fronts . . . On some mornings we can find it hard to get out of bed!

So, however you take your coffee in the morning, be sure to drink it with Jeremiah 29:11. Look again at those words and consider their significance for you, your spouse, and your family.

God Almighty has a future and a hope planned for you. He promises *peace*, which means not merely the absence of war but the presence of His great blessings in your life. God also promises a *future*, an eternal future, where there will be no more crying or pain. We will be able to dwell with our awesome, holy, and perfectly loving Father forever. And this future is not just planned; it's a surefire, bona fide, airtight guarantee!

Yes, in this world—even in your marriage—you will have troubles and tribulations, but Jesus has overcome this world! So take a deep breath, give a big sigh of relief, and thank God for His unwavering promises.

THANK YOU FOR THIS BIG-PICTURE PERSPECTIVE, LORD.
IT'S TOO EASY TO LET THE NEWSPAPER HEADLINES OR
EVEN THE ISSUES ON THE HOME FRONT OVERWHELM.
WE PRAISE YOU FOR THE GOOD PLANS YOU HAVE FOR
YOUR CHILDREN, FOR US. THANK YOU THAT WE CAN
INDEED HOPE IN YOU!

*Assurance
is the fruit that
grows out of the
root of faith.*
STEPHEN
CHARNOCK

LOVE IN ACTION

1. Grab your spouse's hand and head to the beach
or the mountains. Walk in the woods or take in
some stargazing. Go wherever you will be reminded
of how big your God is—and let your spouse's
presence remind you that, even in His bigness, He
knows you intimately and loves you. After all, He
gave you your mate!

2. What saps your hope for the future? Talk, if not
to each other, at least to God about those things.
What can you do to stand strong together and,
more importantly, to stand strong in Him?

DON'T LOSE HEART!

Let us not grow weary while doing good,
for in due season we shall reap if we do not lose heart.
GALATIANS 6:9

I N CASE YOU HAVEN'T noticed, marriage is pretty much a 24/7 undertaking—and we can get physically drained and emotionally spent. And that's one reason why the battle to be the kind of spouse we want to be can get intense.

Every husband and every wife deals with the pressures, whether they stem from demands at the office, demands at home, or both. Buying the groceries, doing the laundry, maintaining the cars, cleaning the house, making the meals, paying the bills—it all takes time. Then add kids to the mix, and the battle to be a good spouse, to not just give our husband or wife the crumbs, rages more furiously.

Yet, we are not to give up. To quote Paul, we are not to "grow weary while doing good." Yes, it is extremely tough to not grow weary, but here's a tip. Often we grow weary at a task when we're trying to do it in our own power. When we are trying to build a Christian marriage—let alone trying to live our Christian life in our own power—we will get beaten down. If we are not in constant communion with Jesus through God's Word and prayer, we are also leaving ourselves vulnerable to the enemy's attacks.

But hear God's awesome promise: "In due season we shall reap if we do not lose heart." As we withstand temptation, prove ourselves faithful, and continue to do good—and we cannot do any of this apart from His grace and strength—we will not only reap the blessings of obedience in this life, but we will enjoy the surpassing glories of spending eternity with our Lord in heaven.

> FATHER, THANK YOU FOR CREATING MARRIAGE. AND
> THANK YOU THAT, OF ALL THE PEOPLE ON THIS PLANET,
> YOU GAVE MY SPOUSE TO ME. LORD, YOU BROUGHT US
> TOGETHER, WHICH MEANS THAT EVEN THOUGH WE'RE
> NOT PERFECT, WE'RE PERFECT FOR EACH OTHER. WE
> KNOW MARRIAGE CAN BE HARD WORK, SO PLEASE HELP
> US BE ALL THE MORE RESOLVED TO LOVE YOU WITH ALL
> OUR HEART SOUL, MIND, AND STRENGTH, BECAUSE THE
> MORE WE LOVE YOU, THE MORE FAITHFULLY WE'LL LOVE
> EACH OTHER. AMEN.

The course of thy life will speak more for thee than the discourse of thy lips.
GEORGE SWINNOCK

LOVE IN ACTION

1. Take a moment to reflect on God's goodness in giving you your spouse. Spend some time in prayer together and, while you're praying, tell the Lord that, no matter what, you are committed to Him and to your marriage—for *life*.

2. Thank your spouse for making it through this entire book with you! Promise each other that you will strive to be the spouse that God wants you to be. Now, give each other the biggest and longest hug you've ever given!

May God richly bless your marriage!
Russ, Brad, and Lisa

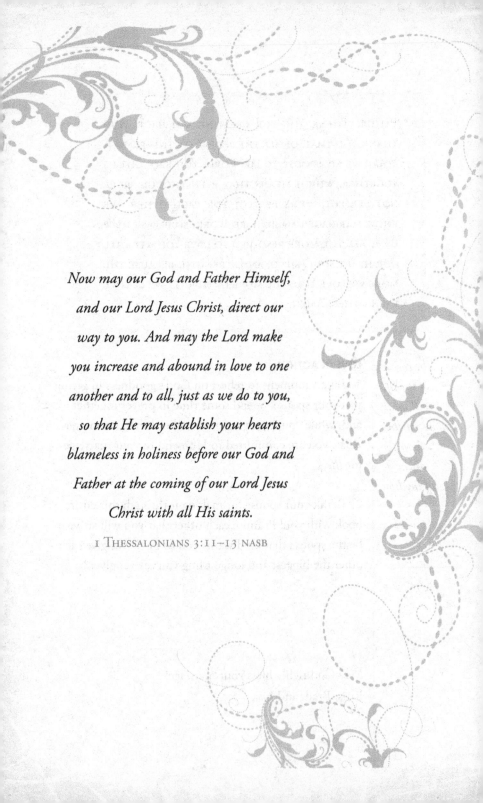

*Now may our God and Father Himself,
and our Lord Jesus Christ, direct our
way to you. And may the Lord make
you increase and abound in love to one
another and to all, just as we do to you,
so that He may establish your hearts
blameless in holiness before our God and
Father at the coming of our Lord Jesus
Christ with all His saints.*

1 THESSALONIANS 3:11–13 NASB

DON'T STOP NOW!

Now that you have grown in your love for each other and for the Lord Jesus Christ, come and be a part of the interactive

No Greater Love community at:

www.NoGreaterLoveChallenge.com.

There you can share your experiences, learn from other's experiences, help others in need, and browse additional marriage and family resources.

TAKE THE CHALLENGE!

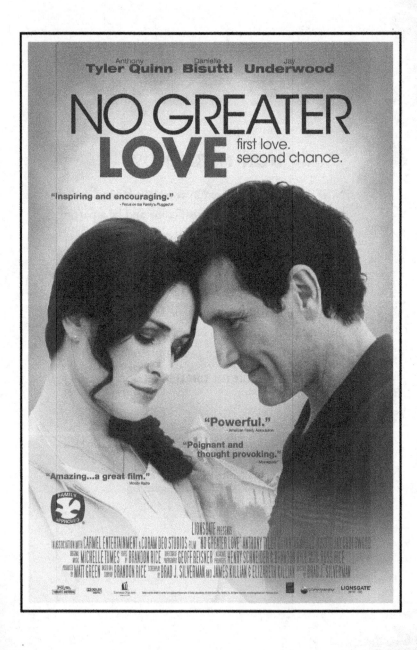

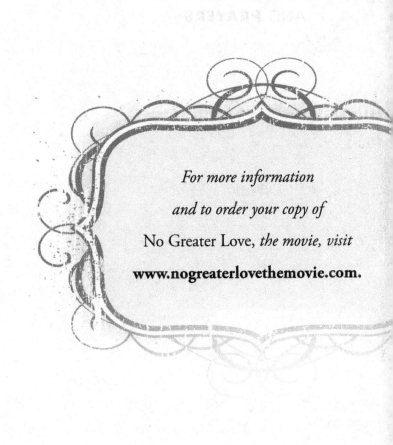

*For more information
and to order your copy of*
No Greater Love, *the movie, visit*
www.nogreaterlovethemovie.com.

PERSONAL NOTES
AND **PRAYERS**